bolivia
A CLIMBING GUIDE

bolivia
A CLIMBING GUIDE

Yossi Brain

THE
MOUNTAINEERS

In memory of Mike Clark (1967–1995)

 Published by
The Mountaineers
1001 SW Klickitat Way, Suite 201
Seattle, WA 98134

© 1999 by Yossi Brain

Published simultaneously in Great Britain by Cordee, 3a DeMontfort Street, Leicester, England, LE1 7HD

Manufactured in the United States of America

Edited by Paula Thurman
Maps and topos by Carmen Julia Arze
All photographs by the author, unless otherwise indicated
Book and cover design by Ani Rucki
Layout by Alice C. Merrill

Cover photograph: *Illampu from Ancohuma, Cordillera Real*
Frontispiece: *Descending the normal route on Huayna Potosí with Charquini, Mururata, and Illimani in the background, Cordillera Real*

Library of Congress Cataloging-in-Publication Data
Brain, Yossi, 1967–
    Bolivia : a climbing guide / Yossi Brain. — 1st ed.
        p.   cm.
    Includes index.
    ISBN 0-89886-495-X
    1. Mountaineering—Bolivia—Guidebooks. 2. Bolivia—Guidebooks.
    I. Title.
GV199.44.B64B726   1999
796.52'2'0984—dc21   98-33320
                                                                    CIP

Contents

Acknowledgments

Thanks to the following climbers with whom I have climbed routes for the first time in Bolivia: Jürgen the German, The Amazing Family Dengg (Austria), Alvaro Garrón and Laura Prömmel (Bolivia), Frank (Germany) and Thomas (Italy), Dr. Helena Martin and Anne Welch, Peter Hutchison (U.K.), Ulli Schatz (Germany), Jason Davis (U.S.), Andy St. Pierre, Gerry "General" Arcari, Mike "Two Dogs" Franklin, Jon Garside (U.K.), Marissa Berndtson (Switzerland), Michael Pennings, Felicia Ennis, David Bandrowski (U.S.), Toto Aramayo (Bolivia), Will Fox (the Hunter S. Thompson of the climbing world), Karl Wolf, Dakin Cook (U.S.), Mark "Pitmaster" Ryle, and Jason "Man of Action" Currie (U.K.) plus Dean Wiggin, Eamonn Flood, Pete Grosset, Archie MacPherson, Andy Macnae (U.K.), Kevin Dougherty (Kenya), John Mudway, Glenn Wilks (U.K.), Marcello Sanguineti and Alessandro Bianchi (Italy) for joining the struggle for new routes and cold beer.

Thanks to the following librarians for their help in locating random bits and pieces of information: Margaret Ecclestone, Alpine Club Library, London; Elsa Claret-Tournier, Bibliothèque de Ecole National de Ski et Alpinisme, Chamonix; and Josep Paytubi, Servei General d'Informació de Muntanya, Sabadell.

For miscellaneous help, thanks to: Carole Jacopini, Dr. John Triplett, formerly head of the U.S. Embassy Medical Unit in La Paz, Liam O'Brien and Mani Herrera of the Defense Mapping Agency in La Paz, Lindsay Griffin, José Velasco, Alvaro Garrón, Andy St. Pierre, Andrew Roberts, Dakin Cook—the motorbike-riding Methodist missionary—for sharing some of his expert knowledge on the Quimsa Cruz and writing the route descriptions for the range, Mario Miranda, Foto Linares, Dennis "Mongo" Moore for writing and revising the Geology section, Fred Hendel, Alex Mitchell, Pete Stewart at Cotswold Shepherds Bush, Gerry Arcari at Rab Carrington, Jim White at Vango, Yves Astier, Paul

Schweizer, John Walmsley, Paul "Result" St. Pierre for help with the Bird section, Jean Steege, and Carla Zapata.

Special thanks to Ulli Schatz, Carmen Julia Arze, and whoever invented e-mail, without which this book would have taken several more years to come out.

The slow walk up—Pete Grosset on the normal route on Illimani, Cordillera Real

Introduction

High mountains, clear cobalt-blue skies virtually every day during the season, no peak fees or added bureaucracy, and easy access to great climbing. Sound good? Welcome to Bolivia! Located in the heart of South America, Bolivia is nearly as big as Alaska or about the same size as France and Spain together. It is the most Indian of the Andean countries, and in economic terms it is one of the poorest countries in the Western Hemisphere. However, the lack of monetary wealth is compensated for by natural if often harsh beauty and an abundance of mountains. There are approximately 1,000 mountains over 5,000 m/16,000 ft, with new routes possible on all of them, and a few mountains of 5,000 m/16,000 ft+ await first ascents in the less-visited areas.

Bolivia is now relatively easy and inexpensive to visit. Having overcome the political and economic chaos of the early 1980s when inflation hit 24,000 percent and governments changed with the seasons, or even more frequently, Bolivia is now economically and politically stable, with one of the lower inflation rates in Latin America. Bolivia is safer in terms of general theft and robbery than neighboring Peru, the climbing is more challenging than in Ecuador, and the weather is far better than in Patagonia. Summarizing a trip to the Cordillera Real in the *Alpine Journal* (1985), Paul Drummond wrote: "The weather was certainly very kind to us, the scenery is stunning and the scale of travelling is small enough to allow short sallies from La Paz . . . once you have cracked the airfare to South America, Bolivia is hard to surpass for economy, convenience and, most of all, character."

A NOTE ABOUT SAFETY

Safety is an important concern in all outdoor activities. No guidebook can alert you to every hazard or anticipate the limitations of every reader.

Therefore, the descriptions of roads, trails, routes, and natural features in this book are not representations that a particular place or excursion will be safe for your party. When you follow any of the routes described in this book, you assume responsibility for your own safety. Under normal conditions, such excursions require the usual attention to traffic, road and trail conditions, weather, terrain, the capabilities of your party, and other factors. Keeping informed on current conditions and exercising common sense are the keys to a safe, enjoyable outing.

The Mountaineers

CHAPTER 1

the cordilleras

The truth is that the mountains are a place where you can find

whatever you want just by looking, as long as you remember that

they do not suffer fools gladly, and particularly dislike those with

preconceived ideas.

Louis de Bernières
The War of Don Emmanuel's Nether Parts, 1990

bolivia's mountain ranges, called *cordilleras* in Spanish, are all in the west of the country on either side of the huge and largely barren Altiplano (literally, "high plain"), which runs from the northwest to the southeast. The plateau is 800 km/500 mi long and 160 km/100 mi wide, with an average altitude of more than 3,500 m/11,500 ft. This makes access to the mountains easy from the capital city of La Paz, situated on the eastern edge of the Altiplano, maximizing the time that can be spent climbing.

Cordillera Apolobamba. Northwest of Illampu is the Cordillera Apolobamba, which stretches northwestward into Peru from Acamani, near Charazani. The cordillera presents some of the best opportunities for sightings of condors. Access from La Paz is either expensive (up to US$400 by jeep) or uncomfortable (up to 24 hours by bus), but the rewards of solitude and the true mountain experience make it all

Summit ridge, Cabeza de Condor, Cordillera Real

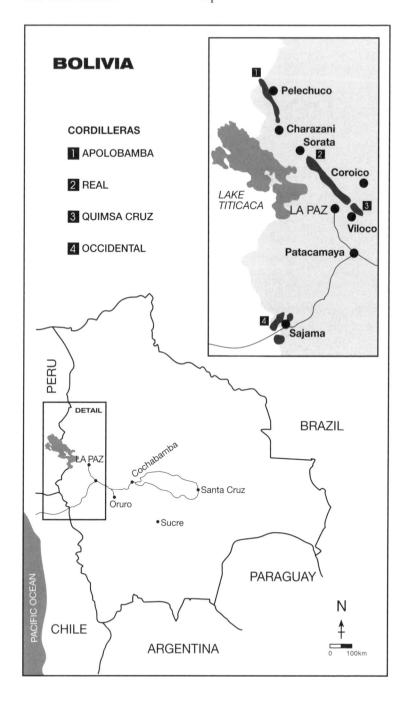

BOLIVIA

CORDILLERAS

1 APOLOBAMBA

2 REAL

3 QUIMSA CRUZ

4 OCCIDENTAL

Pelechuco
Charazani
Sorata
Coroico
LAKE TITICACA
LA PAZ
Viloco
Patacamaya
Sajama

PERU

DETAIL
LA PAZ
Cochabamba
Oruro
Santa Cruz
Sucre

BRAZIL

PARAGUAY

PACIFIC OCEAN

CHILE

ARGENTINA

N

0   100km

worthwhile. Cololo, at 5,915 m/19,406 ft, is the highest peak in the southern Apolobamba (south of Pelechuco); Chaupi Orco, at 6,044 m/19,829 ft and located on the Peruvian border, is the highest peak in the northern Apolobamba.

Cordillera Real. Bolivia's main mountain playground is the Cordillera Real, one of the most impressive mountain groups in the world. It was named the "Royal Range" by the Spanish because of its majestic appearance when seen from the Altiplano. From this vantage point it is possible to see the whole of the 160 km/100 mi range, from Illimani in the southeast to Illampu in the northwest. Austrian climbers later called it "The Himalaya of the New World."

Access to the western side of the cordillera is easy from La Paz. Access to the eastern side is very difficult, where the valleys, the Yungas, drop off steeply toward the jungle of the Amazon basin. Six mountains over 6,000 m/19,600 ft and an estimated 600 over 5,000 m/16,000 ft have routes that range from easy snow plods to extreme technical climbs at high altitude. The Normal Routes on the more popular peaks can be crowded during high season, for example, more than 30 people climbing on the same day, but other peaks are normally climber-free.

Cordillera Quimsa Cruz (Tres Cruces). The deep valley of the Río La Paz separates the Cordillera Quimsa Cruz from the southernmost point of the Cordillera Real—at one point Illimani is 20 km/12 mi from the river and 5,500 m/18,000 ft above it. The highest peak is not, as often stated, Gigante Grande (5,748 m/18,858 ft) but Jacha Cuno Collo (5,800 m/19,029 ft). The elevation of most peaks lies around the 5,400 m/17,500 ft mark. Bolivia's best rock climbing is in the north of the range on granodiorite; the mountains in the south are characterized by beautiful lakeside campsites.

Cordillera Occidental. Distinct from the other three cordilleras is the volcanic Cordillera Occidental, which straddles the border with Chile. Here the mountains stand alone rather than lining up in a chain. Bolivia's highest peak, the extinct and glacier-capped volcano Sajama (6,549 m/21,486 ft), is the only mountain regularly climbed here. The other peaks of the Occidental—including four more over 6,000 m/20,000 ft—are very rarely climbed. Access to the area has improved dramatically with the opening of a new highway linking La Paz with the Chilean coast, reducing the jeep journey to the cordillera from more than 10 hours to under 5 hours.

A CLIMBING HISTORY

Despite the fact that the Incas worshipped mountains as gods, no evidence exists to suggest that Indians climbed in the eastern cordilleras of Bolivia for religious or sacrificial purposes as in other parts of the Andes. Perhaps this is because all the mountains over 5,000 m/ 16,000 ft in the eastern cordilleras are snowcapped. Some of the dry mountains of the Cordillera Occidental near the borders with Chile and Argentina were climbed for the sacrifice of llamas, for example, Licancabur (5,930 m/19,455 ft), and sulfur workings were found near the top of Ollagüe (5,870 m/19,258 ft). Some religion-based fear of mountains remains, along with a legend that an Indian shepherd climbed Illimani, never to return (a fate of many solo climbers in Bolivia). The story goes that he wanted to find the gods, and when he found them, they either turned him into a lump of rock or made him one of them. The absence of climbing activity continued after the Spanish conquest, again, unlike in other Latin American countries such as Ecuador and Peru.

Cordillera Apolobamba

Apart from unconfirmed claims that a Bolivian army captain climbed Palomani Grande in the 1920s, there are no records of climbing in the Apolobamba until 1957, when the first mountaineering expedition arrived. The German group from Berchtesgarten climbed the highest peak in the range, Chaupi Orco (6,044 m/19,829 ft), as well as Huellancollac, Cololo (the second-highest peak), and Huanacuni, among others. They were followed by Italians in 1958, who climbed from the Peruvian side, and then the British Imperial College expedition in 1959, which climbed and thoroughly surveyed the Matchu Suchi Cuchu area to the north of the Pelechuco valley and made the first ascents of Pelechuco Huaracha and Ascarani.

The Japanese Hitotsubashi University expedition in 1961 climbed Chaupi Orco and then moved to the south and climbed Acamani. Their countrymen from Asano High School climbed Cuchillo in 1965 and made a number of other first ascents.

In 1969 the Spanish Manresa expedition made 19 first ascents immediately to the north of the Pelechuco valley, including attaining the summit of a mountain (5,650 m/18,537 ft) at the same time that U.S. astronauts landed on the moon. Hence the peak is called Apollo XI.

Traversing a knife-edged snow arête during the first ascent of the north ridge of Huanacuni, Cordillera Apolobamba

Little of significance was done through the 1970s, but in 1981, an Italian expedition put up some hard routes on Pelechuco Huaracha and Katantica. British groups from the Yorkshire Ramblers Club in 1988 climbed Cololo by its impressive West Ridge and made the second ascent of Nubi. A Bath University expedition climbed Cololo's North Ridge, Nubi, and Palomani Grande (from Peru). A Southampton University expedition climbed Huanacuni and Katantica Oeste in 1992, while the Leeds Mountaineering Club climbed Sunchuli, Iscacuchu, Mita, and Lisa in the same year.

Despite this activity, many first ascents and thousands of new routes await climbers prepared to do the research and suffer the journey to the Apolobamba.

Cordillera Real

Alain Mesili, in his book *La Cordillera Real de los Andes* (1984), mentions a 2-day Spanish attempt on Chacaltaya (5,345 m/17,536 ft) near La Paz in 1610, but apart from this reference, no significant climbing in Bolivia was recorded until May 1877 when French geographer and

17

explorer Charles Wiener attempted Illimani from the southeast, accompanied by Georges de Grumkow, a Bolivian government engineer, and the Peruvian José de Ocampo. The group, supported by one Indian and two mestizo porters, reached the most southeastern of Illimani's peaks at 6,130 m/20,112 ft on May 19 and named the peak Pico de Paris. This was the highest point then reached anywhere in the world, predating Whymper's ascent of Chimborazo (6,310 m/20,702 ft) in Ecuador by more than two years.

On September 9, 1898, the British climber Sir Martin Conway reached the highest of Illimani's peaks, Pico Sur (6,439 m/21,125 ft), with his Swiss-Italian guides Jean-Antoine Maquignaz (son of Jean-Jacques, who made the first ascent of the Matterhorn) and Luigi Pelisier, in spite of being abandoned by their porters. Conway later failed to reach the summit of Ancohuma by 150 m/500 ft. Annie Peck, one of the founders of the American Alpine Club, tried and failed to get sponsorship in her native United States to make the first ascent of Illampu in 1898, although she did make an attempt in 1903 at the age of 53, reaching 5,800 m/19,000 ft.

Climbing in Bolivia was then dominated by Germans and Austrians for 50 years. In 1919 Huayna Potosí and Ancohuma were climbed by Rudolf Dienst and Adolf Schulze. In 1928 the German Hans Pfann, one of the best Alpine climbers of the period, led an expedition that included Austrian Erwin Hein and German Carl Troll, who produced the first map of the Cordillera Real. The expedition made first ascents of Illampu, Casiri, and Chearoco, among others.

Hein stayed on after the expedition left and made the first ascent of Illimani's North Ridge solo. A terse write-up in the *American Alpine Journal* (1929–32) said: "Shortly after the departure of the D.U.O.A.V. expedition a lone German from Sorata made the ascent of Illimani over the north ridge, a new route chosen merely because of its directness from La Paz."

Wilfrid Kühm, a professional mountaineer funded by the official German sports club union, the Leibesübungen, made the first (undisputed) ascent of Sajama with Josef Prem in October 1939 and the first ascent of the Cabeza de Condor at Condoriri in April 1940 (solo, after partner Heinz Gahrmann turned back). However, he is more notorious for planting the Nazi flag on the highest summit of Illimani after the third successful ascent during Easter of 1940 (the first by what is now the Normal Route) with Rolf Boettger and Friedrich Fritz. A photograph of the flag was published in the La Paz newspapers along with accounts of the difficult climb. (The group was caught in a storm and had to spend the night in a snowhole 90 m/300 ft below the summit.)

Edward de la Motte, a British railway engineer living in La Paz and a member of the newly formed Club Andino Boliviano, immediately took 6 days off work, taught Jesús Torres, a Bolivian skier, how to use crampons at the club's ski run at Chacaltaya, and shot off to remove the flag. The Nazi flag was taken down, and on his return to La Paz, Motte told the papers that the climb was easy and suitable for beginners. Torres, a driver at the Club Andino president's brick factory, became the first Bolivian to climb Illimani.

Kühm and Gahrmann fell from the North Ridge while making the first attempt on Illimani's Pico Norte in 1941. Fred Hendel, an anti-Nazi Austrian living in La Paz, organized a rescue despite initial objections from the Club Andino because the climbers and other Germans had re-signed or been expelled from the club following the flag incident. Hendel saw tracks of a fall, but the bodies were never found.

The North Peak of Illimani was reached by Hans Ertl and Gert Schröder on May 6, 1950, after almost 12 hours of climbing on what was until then the hardest climb done in Bolivia. Both climbers suffered frostbitten toes.

Ertl was a photographer and cameraman. He invented the first un-derwater camera, which was used in the 1936 Olympics in Berlin, and he skied off the high jump to film the experience. He was also a lead-ing climber before the Second World War, cycling for days to climb hard routes in the Alps. In 1934 he was a member of the Dyhrenfurth Broad Peak expedition, and in 1953 he filmed the exhausted Hermann Buhl staggering back back down from Nanga Parbat after Buhl's solo climb.

During World War II, Ertl was Field Marshal Rommel's personal photographer. After the war, he was accused of glorifying the Nazis through his work, and he was unable to get a job in Germany. He has always denied being a member of the Nazi party. Through friends of friends, Ertl met Bishop Udal at the Vatican, and he helped Ertl leave Europe. Udal also helped Klaus Barbie, the Butcher of Lyons.

Ertl arrived in Puna de Atacama in Chile where he was asked if he wanted to go to Peru or Bolivia. He chose Bolivia, met up with a German expedition, and was given such a welcome at La Paz station on March 3, 1950, including being met by the then Bolivian President Urriolagoitia, that the U.S., British, French, and Russian embassies made formal protests.

In addition to Ertl's first ascent of Pico Norte of Illimani, he made the second ascent of Illampu, the third ascents of Sajama and Cabeza de Condor, and he put up a new route on Ancohuma, the Northwest Ridge.

Ertl never recovered mentally from the death of his daughter Monica. Monica was a communist and the lover of Inti Peredo, a revolutionary who survived fighting with Che Guevara in Che's disastrous Bolivia campaign in 1967, but who was later murdered in 1969. Monica killed the Bolivian Consul to Hamburg, Quintanilla, in the late 1960s because he had been one of the leading organizers of the hunt for Che. On her return to Bolivia, Monica was murdered by the Bolivian secret services—Ertl claimed with the involvement of Klaus Barbie—and her body was dumped in the La Paz suburb of El Alto.

Ertl still lives in Bolivia as a recluse on a plot of land 300 km/188 mi from the city of Santa Cruz in the lowlands.

A Mexican expedition in 1960 made various first ascents in the Condoriri area along with Bolivians Alfredo Martínez and Douglas Moore. They named all the peaks they climbed with no reference to local custom, so it is difficult to tell exactly which mountains were climbed.

In 1962 a British group from Reading University made 20 first ascents in the Negruni area and also climbed Chearoco. The Alpine Club of the Tokyo University of Foreign Studies' 1964 expedition climbed 11 peaks in the Vinowara Group between the Negruni Group and Chachacomani. During the same year, a Yugoslavian expedition made 10 first ascents in the Condoriri area.

In 1966 another British university group, this time from University College Bangor, made 15 first ascents in the until-then unexplored area between Ancohuma and Negruni. Tragically, the expedition leader, Michael Birchall, was killed while descending Casiri Este. The Negruni Group was visited again in 1969 by Germans from the Bayerische Naturfreunde, who made 16 first ascents followed by another 8 in the Checapa area. A German group from Regensburg made 24 first ascents in and around the Negruni Group in 1971, followed by a 6-day, 2½ km/1½ mi traverse of the Northeast Ridge of Illampu.

The only recorded incident of climbing under fire in Bolivia happened in 1969 while a Spanish group from Manresa was putting up a new route on the North Ridge of Pico Norte on Illimani. José María Montfort, in the *American Alpine Journal* (1970–71), wrote: "As we pitched Camp II [5,600 m/18,375 ft], we were challenged by an armed patrol far below on the eastern glacier. On the morning of the 11th [August] we heard bullets whistle past. Luckily clouds came in and we could continue to place camp." The Spaniards believed the attack was because the soldiers thought they were looking for a plane loaded with gold that had crashed into the mountain in 1938.

The imposing 1,000 m/3,300 ft West Face of Huayna Potosí was first climbed by its West Ridge in 1969 by North Americans John Hudson and Roman Laba. The first proper route up the face was done the next year by Dobbs Harthorne, Andy Harvard, James Lanney, and Todd Thompson (U.S.). The West Face of Huayna Potosí has since become a trade route and has been guided on a number of occasions.

The biggest single climbing accident in Bolivia happened in 1989 as a group of six Chileans returned to high camp on Illimani having completed the Normal Route. Five were killed by a fall and a sixth, who survived the fall, died of exposure before rescuers arrived.

In April 1991 two Yugoslavs climbed Alpos Secret (VI+/ED3) on Illampu's West Face, and later that year, in June, two groups of Yugoslavs climbed two 1,000 m/3,300 ft routes on the same face at V+/ED and VI/ED2. These are the hardest recorded routes in the history of climbing in Bolivia.

Cordillera Quimsa Cruz

The first recorded climbing in the Quimsa Cruz was in 1903–04 in the Araca area to the north by the Austrian Henry Hoek, who climbed Chancapiña (5,260 m/17,257 ft).

In 1911 Theodor Herzog and Carl Seelig walked from the north to the south of the range along the western side and got to within 20 m/65 ft of the highest peak in the cordillera, the 5,800 m/19,029 ft Jacha Cuno Collo. The two Germans also made the first ascent of Korichuma, also called Immaculado.

Adolf Schulze, the first person up Huayna Potosí and Ancohuma, along with Rudolf Dienst, climbed the 5,400 m/17,716 ft rock tower El Yunque in 1915 with E. Overlack.

Bolivia-based German Wilfrid Kühm and Austrian Josef Prem, who climbed Sajama together in 1939, also made a trip to the Quimsa Cruz that year and made a number of first ascents, including Huayna Cuno Collo (5,640 m/18,504 ft). They were the first to reach the summit of Jacha Cuno Collo.

A Japanese expedition in 1968 made 13 first ascents, but there is confusion about exactly which peaks were climbed. In 1969 a German expedition under Rudi Knott climbed extensively in the Araca area. Italians under Santino Calegari made a number of first ascents and the second ascent of Gigante Grande in 1974.

In 1987 a German expedition, which also included José Miranda and four other Bolivians, rock climbed extensively in the Araca and Choquetanga areas, producing a detailed, well-mapped expedition report. Activity through the 1990s has been based mainly around rock climbing, with the most significant snow/ice route being the West Face of Gigante Grande, climbed first by an Argentinian/Spanish group in 1993 and a few weeks later by a U.S. team. *American Alpine Journal* contributor Evelio Echevarría (U.S.) has made nine trips to the Quimsa Cruz, mainly solo; Bolivia-based U.S. Methodist missionary and climber Dakin Cook has made repeated trips to the area by motorbike and more recently by Volkswagen bus.

Cordillera Occidental

Some of the dry southern peaks near the border with Argentina were climbed by local peoples during the nineteenth century, if not earlier. The first recorded ascent of Licancabur (5,930 m/19,455 ft) was in 1884, but pre-Hispanic remains were found on top; similarly, the first ascent of Ollagüe (5,870 m/19,258 ft) is dated as 1888, but sulfur workings are located near the top.

The first significant recorded climbing in the area was done by Josef Prem, an Oruro-based Austrian mining engineer, who climbed Parinacota in 1928 with a Bolivian known simply as Terán. Prem described Sajama as a hobby of his—his record of attempts suggests it was more of an obsession. He soloed the Northwest Ridge to about 6,200 m/20,350 ft in 1927, and then went back in 1931 with W. Stricker and got to within 250 m/820 ft of the summit via the Northwest Ridge before being halted by a thunderstorm.

In August 1939 Prem returned with the Italian Piero Ghiglione and went back up the Northwest Ridge. Prem stated they turned back

100–150 m/300–500 ft below the summit because of bad snow conditions—fresh snow on top of spiky *nieve penitentes*—while Ghiglione
claimed to have reached the summit. (Fred Hendel, in *Mountains in
Bolivia* [1992], relates another tale about Ghiglione in Bolivia: Friedrich
Fritz and Ghiglione attempted Illimani. Hendel writes: "The weather
turned bad and they did not make it to the top, but Ghiglione tried to
convince Fritz to join him in claiming that they did reach the top. Fritz
refused in spite of Ghiglione's efforts . . . Ghiglione later wrote in an
Italian newspaper that they had reached the top.")

Finally, in October 1939, Prem attempted Sajama via the Southeast
Ridge with Wilfrid Kühm and made the summit in clear weather. Unfortunately, his fingers were frostbitten while taking pictures with his mit-
tens off in the hurricane-force wind.

Little of significance has been done in the Cordillera Occidental
since the first ascents, although there is potential for some hard, high-
altitude early-season ice lines on Sajama's West Face, and some of the
more southerly mountains await exploration.

Bolivian Climbers

The vast majority of significant climbing in Bolivia has been done by
Europeans and North Americans, either on expeditions or based in
Bolivia. Edward de la Motte, in the *Alpine Journal* (1940), described
mountaineering as being "a cult in Bolivia with few worshippers." More
than 40 years later, little had changed according to Stanley Shepard, a
U.S. citizen living in La Paz, who wrote in the *American Alpine Journal*
(1981): "At the moment, La Paz has one weekend climber: me. I solo
a lot."

Bolivians made a number of significant first ascents during the
golden age of the Club Andino in the first decade of its existence. However, what records were kept have been lost, and it is very difficult to find
out what was climbed.

On August 1, 1947, club members led by German resident Friedrich
Fritz made the first ascent of Chachacomani (6,074 m/19,928 ft). The
previous year, in March 1946, Friedrich Ahlfeld led a group in the first
ascent of Gigante Grande (5,748 m/18,858 ft) in the Quimsa Cruz, taking snow from the top of the mountain back to La Paz to make the club's
"Cocktail de cumbre." Both ascents used skis to get into and out from
the routes.

René Zalles and Edmundo García claimed the first ascent of

Pomerata (6,222 m/20,413 ft) in the Cordillera Occidental in May 1946 and described their climb in the *Boletín* of the Club Andino (no. 3, August 1946). In 1974 the *American Alpine Journal* stated without further explanation that "claims for the first ascent are generally disbelieved." Doubts about this ascent appear to stem from remarks made to the Andean historian Evelio Echevarría while in Bolivia in 1953. Chileans Sergio Kunstmann and Claudio Meier then claimed the first ascent of the mountain on October 11, 1964.

Ascents of Tiquimani in the Cordillera Real were made by club members in 1941 and then by a Bolivian army group led by Major Azero in April 1963. Records do not appear to have survived for either climb. Other mountains climbed by the club included Illimani, Huayna Potosí, Mururata, Takesi, and María Lloco.

The Club Andino, founded in 1939, built the road to Chacaltaya, where the club also built the first ski lift in South America. The first president of the club, Raúl Posnansky, was killed in this area in an avalanche in July 1943, although given the level of glacial retreat this is hard to imagine now. The initial enthusiasm for climbing in the club lasted through the 1950s and 1960s, but very few records survive, so it is difficult to tell which peaks were climbed or attempted. Club members Alfredo Martínez, who started climbing in 1953, and Ronnie Ibatta accompanied a number of foreign expeditions during the 1960s, making a number of first ascents in the Apolobamba, Quimsa Cruz, and Condoriri. Ernesto Sánchez carried on the tradition during the 1970s, although his climbing was much harder than his predecessors' until his death on Illimani in 1975. His main partner was the French climber Alain Mesili. Together they climbed Illampu's East Face Direct (III/D-) and Pico Gorra de Hielo Directisima (II/AD) at Illampu in 1970. In 1972 they made the first ascent of the Vía Khoya Khoyu (III/D-), the obvious triangle face on the west side of Illimani. In August that year they did the three-peak traverse of Illimani in 6 days, climbed the South Face of Pico Norte and then skied down it—the first extreme ski descent in Bolivia. In 1973 they traversed Pico Schulze, Pirámide Sur, and the Northeast Face of Illampu (III/D-) and also climbed the Southwest Face of Huayna Illampu (IV+/TD) plus the South Pyramid (III/D-) on Pico Schulze's Southeast Face. In 1974 they did the First Pillar on Illampu's East Face (IV/D+); Mesili returned the next year to do the Second Pillar (IV/D+).

Camp below Tiquimani, Cordillera Real

Illimani at dawn from the southeast (Photo by Dakin Cook)

Born in Paris in 1949, Alain Mesili moved to Bolivia in 1969 where he has done more than any other climber to push the standard of climbing in the country. Other significant routes Mesili climbed without Sánchez include the Vía del Triangulo (III/D-) on Huayna Potosí's 1,000 m/3,300 ft West Face in 1971, the beautiful Cabeza de Condor Directisima (IV/D+) at Condoriri in 1973, and the first ascent of the Vía de los Franceses on Huayna Potosí in 1974 (II/AD)—the best route on the East Face. In one week at Condoriri in September 1976 he made two solo first ascents: Huallomen (III/D-, but now rated VI/ED1+ due to changing conditions) and the first gully on Ala Derecha (IV+/TD). In 1978 he made the first ascent of the hard satellite peak of Huayna Potosí, named Pico Mesili, by a IV/D+ route and two routes on the South Face of Illimani (IV/TD and III/D-). In 1979 he climbed Ala Izquierda South Face (III/D-) at Condoriri, and in 1982 he climbed the Principal Pillar (IV/D+) in the East Face of Pico del Norte at Illampu.

These routes were a generation ahead of virtually everything else that had been done in Bolivia until then. Mesili's routes pushed local climbers to new standards while also encouraging foreign climbers to visit and put up hard routes at high altitude.

In 1984 Mesili's *La Cordillera Real de los Andes* was published, the first proper climbing guidebook to the country. It includes topos and descriptions of many of the routes he climbed. Mesili's personal collection of climbing notes and records, the most comprehensive materials ever collected on mountaineering and exploring in Bolivia, were confiscated in 1990 when Mesili became a suspect in the bombing of the U.S. marines' house in the Miraflores part of La Paz.

Mesili fled Bolivia, and after nearly four years on the run in the United States, he was arrested in 1994 and then held in a series of jails before being returned to Bolivia in 1995 in a prisoner exchange between the two governments. Mesili was held for another two and a half years in the Chonchocoro prison until his release without charge in 1997. His ordeal had come to an end, but his detailed climbing records were never returned.

The other expatriate climber in Bolivia who made a big impact was Stan Shepard, a U.S. citizen. Shepard did not climb as hard as Mesili, but he climbed rock and ice whenever and wherever he could, encouraging young Bolivians to climb as well. His favorite area was the Quimsa Cruz, which he first visited by motorbike in 1967. In 1991 he led a rock-climbing expedition which climbed the impressive 4,850 m/15,912 ft granite needle of Pico Pene (5.10a/VI+). Shepard was killed in 1993 on the way to a rescue in the Quimsa Cruz when the jeep he was driving slipped off the road in snow and plummeted down a cliff.

Today, Bolivia has some very good amateur climbers. They tend to concentrate on rock climbing because it is more accessible, a necessity given the Bolivian practice of working on Saturday mornings and the very low incidence of private car ownership. Bolivian guides work solidly through the climbing season, so the majority do not appear to have time to explore new routes.

HIGHLAND GEOLOGY

Bolivia's mountains over 4,000 m/13,000 ft are found in the Cordilleras Occidental and Oriental (split into the Apolobamba, Real, and Quimsa Cruz ranges) on either side of the Altiplano. The mountain ranges trend approximately northwest to southeast.

The Cordillera Occidental occupies the border with Chile and is composed of Cenozoic (65 million years ago to the present) volcanoes, domes, flows, ignimbrites (huge, hot ash flows—you wouldn't want to be around when one erupts), and sedimentary rocks derived from these volcanics. The main phase of volcanism was about 25 to 22 million years ago during the Miocene period.

The Altiplano contains many salt lakes *(salares)*, including the larg-est of them all, the Salar de Uyuni. The western cordillera hosts fumerolic sulfur and borate deposits; the eastern cordilleras contain hundreds of historic polymetallic vein-hosted mineral deposits that were exploited principally for silver. In the western cordillera, the main eco-nomic activity of the region is the exploitation of borates (some are used for soap) from lake deposits in the southern part of the cordillera, al-though numerous mining companies are exploring the altered strato-volcanoes for gold and silver. Tourism in the far south of the cordillera near Lagunas Colorado and Verde is a recent but significant phenom-enon that can only be explained by the area having been described in one guidebook as one of the most desolate areas in South America.

There have been no volcanic eruptions recorded within Bolivia, and only one of the Bolivian volcanoes is classified as active, the 5,870 m/19,258 ft Ollagüe southwest of Uyuni, where a very active fumarole can usually be seen venting gases on its southern flank. The volcanoes in the area around Sajama are very recent with well-formed summit craters. Although they are not considered active, they are by no means extinct.

The Altiplano is an elongated basin between the two main mountain ranges, and it stretches from southern Peru to North Lipez, south of the Salar de Uyuni. In the recent geological past (that is, only millions of years ago), the Altiplano was a giant canyon, or fracture, which has since been filled with sediments derived from the two cordilleras. At the end of the last Ice Age, the area hosted a large inland sea of which Lakes Titicaca, Poopo, Coipasa, and Uyuni are the remnants.

Historically, the Altiplano has been the center of human settlement in Bolivia, with various thriving pre-Columbian cultures, such as the Inca, Tiawanaku, Chiripa, and Wankarani. The major roads and north–south transportation routes lie within the Altiplano, and the city of La Paz is found on the eastern edge nestled in a canyon formed by rivers flowing off the Altiplano.

The eastern Cordillera Oriental includes three major cordilleras with peaks over 6,000 m/20,000 ft—Real, Apolobamba, and Quimsa Cruz—and a score of lesser ranges to the south. These are composed primarily of sedimentary rocks from the Paeleozoic and Mesozoic eras (600–225 million and 225–65 million years ago, respectively), with occasional more recent intrusive and volcanic centers. The rocks run the gamut of sedimentary rocks, including sandstones, siltstones, shales, limestones, and quartzites. Volumetrically and economically, Ordovician and Silurian shales and siltstones are probably the most important sequences (formed 500–440 million and 440–395 million years ago, respectively).

The cordillera is a classic locality in which to study structural and sedimentary geology: several cataclysmic episodes of deformation have helped form it, and low-angle thrust faults occur throughout the area. (This type of fault decapitates entire ranges and moves massive amounts of rock several kilometers.)

The Cordillera Oriental is the area of historic metallic mining of past centuries, and it is one of the most strongly mineralized mountain chains in the world, referred to as a metallogenic province. The mines and deposits show strong mineralogic zoning with a wide, heavily exploited tin-silver belt running down the western side of the cordillera. A parallel gold-antimony belt just east of the classic tin-silver belt is flanked on the far eastern side by a wide lead-zinc-silver belt. These belts are only tens of kilometers wide but are hundreds of kilometers long, running northwest to southeast. A number of theories have been been proposed as to the cause of this zoning, but it has not been fully explained.

The highest peaks of the Cordillera Oriental, such as Illimani, Illampu, and Huayna Potosí, are intrusive massifs (primarily granodiorite) punched up through the sediments during the Cenozoic era (65 million years ago to the present). Intrusive rocks such as granite and granodiorite are much more resistant to erosion than the shales and siltstones and therefore usually form the cores of the highest mountains. The entire Quimsa Cruz range is composed of granodiorite forming a towering massif over the surrounding sedimentary rocks.

NATURAL HISTORY

Although nothing appears to live above the snow line, climbers heading to and from the mountains will see many distinctively Bolivian and Andean animals and birds. This brief roundup describes some of the more visible and unusual species that inhabit areas close to the mountains.

Mammals

The most visible highland animals are the camelids—llamas, alpacas, and vicuñas—the biggest native South American mammals, which live at altitudes of up to 5,500 m/18,000 ft.

Llamas were domesticated thousands of years ago. They are used primarily for meat (which is very low in cholesterol), wool, and also as pack animals—a large llama can carry 40 kgs/88 lbs or more.

With their big round eyes and woolly coats, llamas look cuddly, but they seem to be in a permanently bad mood. When annoyed, they flatten their ears and spit—sometimes to distances farther than 10 m/ 30 ft. They fight by standing on their hind legs and neck-wrestling each other, trying to get a grip on one another's ears—llamas without ears are a relatively common sight. They chase each other and try to bite the hind legs of the other to bring it down. They will also chase off dogs.

Alpacas are smaller than llamas and have smaller noses and thicker coats, which tend to be a uniform dark brown, almost black, color compared to the predominantly white with brown/black of the llamas. Alpacas provide high-quality wool, but they are not eaten as often as llamas and are not used as pack animals. Alpacas are more particular about what they eat and tend to stay near wetter pastures.

Vicuñas (*huari* in Aymara) are smaller than llamas and alpacas, and their hair is much shorter—they look more like antelope than the others. They do not spend their lives in herds like the other Bolivian camelids but in families of 2 to 12, with one male adult *(macho)* leading female adults *(hembras)* and youngsters *(jovenes)*. Single males live in separate groups, which tend to be much larger, 10 to 60 strong.

Vicuña wool is extremely fine. Because vicuñas do not breed in captivity, they have never been domesticated. As a result, they are hunted. Estimates suggest there were more than 1 million vicuñas in Bolivia during pre-Inca times, but this number fell steadily after the Spanish arrived. The first laws to protect vicuñas in Bolivia were passed in 1918, but by the 1950s their numbers were down to 400,000, and in 1965 only 6,000 were left. The area now covered by the Reserva Nacional de Fauna Ulla Ulla to the west of the Cordillera Apolobamba counted 97 vicuñas in 1965. There are now more than 6,000 vicuñas in the reserve and a total of 12,000 in the country. It is illegal to kill vicuñas, but illicit hunting still goes on. Outside Ulla Ulla, the other main place you are likely to see them is in the Cordillera Occidental around Sajama.

Viscachas are cat-sized rodents with bushy, squirrel-like tails. They live in colonies in rocks near water, lakes, or streams, and they leap like kangaroos, using their overdeveloped back legs. The best time to see them is at sunrise and sunset, when they enjoy the first and last warmth of the day. They are shot and eaten by locals, who also use their fur for clothing.

On the eastern slopes of the eastern cordilleras it is possible in theory to see bespectacled bears *(oso anteojos)*, although they are extremely rare and endangered. Another rare inhabitant of this area is the puma, which is important in native mythology. Pumas are held to be powerful physically and spiritually. Their spirits are invoked at important ceremonies, and their skins fetch a lot of money. Pumas are hard to see because they hunt alone at night and move quickly and silently. They have also been spotted in the Sajama and Ulla Ulla areas.

Andean foxes *(zorro andino)* are smaller than their European and North American counterparts and look more like coyotes than the average fox.

Wild armadillos *(quirquincho)* are endangered. Native to the Altiplano south of La Paz and still seen in the Sajama area, they are hunted to make the bodies of *charangos,* traditional small, guitarlike instruments, and stuffed for souvenirs.

Wild chinchillas have been hunted to extinction in Bolivia for their coats—there have been no reported sightings in 50 years. Until 1900, Bolivia exported 500,000 chinchilla skins annually to Chile, which, considering the weight and size of the animals, made them the most expensive skins in the world. Chinchillas used to live in the Cordillera Occidental.

Birds
Bolivia is the seventh richest country on the planet for birds. Of the 1,358 bird species so far identified in Bolivia (43 percent of all species found in South America), 120 species are found in the Altiplano and Andes regions of the country.

Condors, important in pre-Hispanic mythology and the modern national symbol, avoid areas of human habitation, but they can be seen in many mountain areas, especially on the eastern side of the eastern cordilleras and in the Apolobamba. Condors are spectacularly big with wingspans of up to 3 m/10 ft—the largest of any land bird. The huge wings are not flapped while in flight—the great birds circle upward riding the thermals. The image of grace and power that condors project when in the air is lost upon landing—they hop around in a clumsy, uncoordinated way. They gorge themselves on carrion to such an extent that they cannot fly until they have digested the feast, making them easy targets for hunters who bait them with carcasses, lie in wait, and then pounce after the birds have eaten. (Hunting condors is illegal.) They have a white ruff and their red heads are bald, which makes them easier to clean after a carcass-stripping session.

The mountain caracara *(María)* is another scavenger, and the most beautiful bird regularly seen in the highlands. It has a yellow beak, red face, black upperparts and neck, white underparts, and yellow claws. The birds come to camps to hunt for scraps and are often seen along roadsides waiting for roadkill. On seeing a María bird, superstitious Bolivians say *"Suerte María"* three times to bring luck for the journey.

High Andean lakes, rivers, and marshes support a variety of birds. The black-and-white Andean goose *(ganzo andino* or *huallata)* spends much of its time in pairs (they mate for life). At times they are very, very noisy but not as noisy as Andean gulls *(gaviota Andina)*. These gulls live on surprisingly high lakes and have even been seen over the summit of Huayna Potosí at 6,088 m/19,974 ft. Andean lapwings *(leki)* blend into their surroundings until they take off and display striking V-shaped, white wing flashes. The rare Diademed sandpiper is found above 4,000 m/13,000 ft. Torrent ducks *(pato de torrentes/de las torrenteras)* have an amazing ability to swim against the current in fast-flowing streams, and they rarely fly. They are seen on the eastern side of the eastern cordilleras, including the Pelechuco valley in Apolobamba, but they are endangered because of deforestation, mining pollution of rivers, and competition for food with trout, which were artificially introduced to Bolivia at the start of the twentieth century and are doing very well.

One of the more bizarre sights in Bolivia is the pink flamingos that live on the shores of Lake Titicaca and also in salty lakes near Sajama and in the far southwest of the country. Three types of flamingos are found in Bolivia: the endangered Andean (*Parina Grande*), the more common Chilean (*Flamenco Chileno*), and Puna or James (*Parina Chica*), which was assumed to be extinct until 1957. The continued existence of the Andean and James flamingos is threatened by mining pollution of lakes and egg collection. Feathers from juvenile flamingos are used to stuff sleeping bags, and in the Oruro region flamingo *(charque de pariguana)* is served in some restaurants.

Dovelike seedsnipes are often found in small groups throughout the

Altiplano and high Andean zones. When disturbed, they fly off in a whir of wings emitting a soft whistling sound. Tinamou *(perdiz)* look and behave like Scottish ptarmigans, squawking loudly and flapping furiously to fly away when they are surprised. The birds are the size of chickens but apparently taste better.

Many smaller birds are found in the highlands. Ground tyrants perch until they chase insects. The thrush-sized, wing-barred Cincloides is often found near watercourses where it searches for insects. Sierra finches and siskins are seen on the ground looking for seeds; the white-winged Duica finch, with gray upperparts and breast and white throat, belly, and wing bars is found up to the snow line. The piping calls of Rockcreepers and Canasteros give away the presence of species that would otherwise go unnoticed. Other surprisingly high flyers are hummingbirds *(picaflores* or *colibris)*, which are found over 4,000 m/13,000 ft. To survive the low nighttime temperatures, the Andean hillstar drops its body temperature from 39.5° C/103° F to 15° C/59° F and its heart rate from 1,200 beats per minute to 40 beats per minute.

Flora

From a layperson's perspective, the Altiplano is pretty bleak in terms of vegetation, which mainly consists of scrubby bushes and scrubby grass, apart from cultivated plants. Two hundred varieties of potato are grown in Bolivia along with other tubers, plus the high-protein quinoa grain.

The coarse grass that grows in clumps and is eaten by llamas is called *ichu; thola* and *yareta* grasses are used for fuel. On the shores of Lake Titicaca, *totora* reed grass grows, which is used in the construction of traditional *bolsa* boats. It was also used by the Norwegian explorer Thor Heyerdahl for his boat *Kon-Tiki*, which was built on the Bolivian side of the lake.

The Altiplano around La Paz was covered in small bushes 40 years ago, but these have been cut down and used for firewood. Trees are rare, as they take a long time to grow in the dry Altiplano but not much time to chop down. Most trees are eucalyptus, a non-native, water-guzzling species that, like trout, is thriving to the detriment of native species. The main exception to this is in the area between Sajama and the Payachatas in the Cordillera Occidental, where the red-barked *keñua* trees are surviving in large numbers. The stubby bushlike trees grow at the highest altitudes in the world, up to 5,000 m/16,000 ft.

preparations

To a wanderer in a snow covered field, a dried up prune or an old

crust of bread tasted more delicious than a whole meal here with the

prosperous guildsmen.

Hermann Hesse
Narcissus and Goldmund, 1930

La Paz is the world's highest capital city and one of the most impressively sited cities on the planet. It is also one of the most Indian cities in the Andes. The entire city of 800,000 nestles in a giant canyon with the triple-peaked Illimani, 6,439 m/21,125 ft, providing a stunning backdrop. The airport is at 4,058 m/13,313 ft, the center (Plaza Murillo) at 3,660 m/12,008 ft, while the southern suburbs stretch down below 3,300 m/10,800 ft. The poor live in the area around the airport in what is now the separate city of El Alto, one of the fastest growing cities in Latin America, which has an official population of 400,000 and an actual population closer to double that. The rich live below the center in the Zona Sur, "the South Zone," where it is warmer. The differences between El Alto and the Zona Sur are staggering. In El Alto you are somewhere in the Third World; in the Zona Sur you could be in an wealthy suburb of a major U.S. city.

However, it's not the scenery that takes your breath away on arrival—it's the lack of air.

Illampu from the main square in Sorata, Cordillera Real

GETTING THERE

Most air routes from North America to La Paz go through Miami. From Europe there is a greater choice, with route possibilities via the United States or any of the major South American cities. Weight allowances vary among airlines and tend to be much higher with North American airlines; stopover requirements also vary. So a more expensive ticket might end up costing less than a cheaper ticket plus excess baggage and stopover costs. Check with several airlines before purchasing your ticket.

The US$20 departure tax on all international flights at La Paz airport is payable in dollars or bolivianos.

VISAS

Tourists get a 30-day (and sometimes 90-day) visa free of charge upon entry in Bolivia. If you need longer—up to a total of 90 days—go to the immigration office on Calle Camacho and Calle Loayza in La Paz before the 30 days are up. European Union citizens can get an extra 60 days free of charge; U.S. citizens and some others pay US$20 for each extra 30 days.

ACCLIMATIZATION

Don Emmanuel explained to the people. "You will all be ill for a while because there is less air up here to breathe. If you think you are dying, do not be deceived, you will soon feel better. Each of you must find their own way to deal with it. Some people eat a great deal and drink a lot of alcohol, but for others this only makes the soroche even worse, so they have to eat and drink very little. Again, some people should get used to it by keeping busy, and others should lie in the dark and do nothing."

Louis de Bernières
The War of Don Emmanuel's Nether Parts, 1990

The Bolivian Andes are considerably higher than the Rockies or the Alps, and acclimatization is essential before attempting any of the peaks. Fitness is no substitute for acclimatization; indeed, fit young men appear to have more problems than other people.

The majority of people feel ill on arrival in La Paz. This is commonly called *soroche*. Visitors occasionally collapse while carrying their luggage from the arrival lounge of the airport. Common symptoms of mild altitude sickness include breathlessness, a racing pulse, lethargy, tiredness, inability to sleep, loss of appetite, headache, and dehydration. These symptoms normally last for a couple of days.

The U.S. Embassy in La Paz recommends that people who fly directly to the city's 4,058 m/13,313 ft airport from sea level should take acetazolamide (Diamox) prophylactically—preferably via sustainable-release tablets. Acetazolamide speeds up acclimatization by acidifying the blood, which increases respiration. It improves oxygen transport and helps improve sleep. Acetazolamide works directly to prevent or reduce High Altitude Pulmonary Edema and helps prevent High Altitude Cerebral Edema (see the section "Medical Issues"). The drug acts as a diuretic, so more clear liquids (no alcohol) should be drunk while taking it. Acetazolamide sometimes causes a tingling sensation in the fingers and toes, and it should not be taken by people with sulfur allergies. Talk with your doctor about acetazolamide, and if you plan to use it for the first time, try some well before your trip to check that there are no unpleasant side effects.

Note: There is no medical evidence that "Sorojchi" pills, on sale in La Paz and given out by some of the hotels, have any impact on altitude sickness. Similarly, there is no medical evidence that the traditional coca tea helps beyond alleviating dehydration and being a very mild painkiller.

No one knows for sure what causes altitude sickness, but the key to avoiding it seems to be to take it really easy when you arrive. People who rush their acclimatization invariably regret it later. La Paz is at 3,100–4,100 m/10,200–13,400 ft depending on where you are—the center is at 3,600 m/11,800 ft. Do nothing on your first day in La Paz. Just lie down, and let your body get on with adapting. Day two can be spent moving around slowly or taking a bus or jeep to Tiwanaku or Copacabana for a bit of sightseeing.

When you arrive, your body must adapt to the lower pressure, which means you must breathe 50 percent more often than at sea level to get the same amount of oxygen into your blood. As a consequence, you lose a lot of water through breathing in the dry air, so you must consciously drink much more water than at sea level. (Bottled mineral water is widely available in La Paz.) Above 5,000 m/16,000 ft, you need more than 5 liters/quarts a day. Check the color of your urine: in the words of altitude expert Charles Houston, M.D., it should be "gin clear"; the more yellow the urine, the more dehydrated you are. In addition, eat light meals that are high in carbohydrates and low in fat.

Full acclimatization to the height of La Paz involves increasing your red blood cell count by 50 percent and takes about five months. However, a week at the height of La Paz or the Altiplano is normally sufficient before climbing above 5,000 m/16,000 ft. You could spend this time trekking on the Isla del Sol, visiting the Salar de Uyuni, or doing a high-altitude trek with llamas or mules carrying the kit. Most (but not all) climbers will then be ready to go. However, it is still possible to get altitude sickness if you ascend faster than your body is capable of adjusting. Unfortunately, these physiological differences cannot be foreseen —individuals react in different ways and at different rates to high altitudes.

SPANISH

You will need to know some Spanish to get around in Bolivia. Outside of tourist agencies and some hotels, little English is spoken or understood in La Paz and none at all in the countryside. It is a good idea to learn how to count, tell time, and say the days of the week in Spanish before coming to Bolivia; it will make shopping and arranging transportation easier.

You might meet people in the countryside *(campo)* who do not speak any Spanish but only one of the native languages: Aymara in the Cordillera Real, Quimsa Cruz, and Occidental, and Quechua in the Cordillera Apolobamba. However, Aymara speakers normally count in Spanish, and if your pronunciation is close enough, place names are the same.

FOOD

At high altitudes the body does not process fat and protein as efficiently as at lower altitudes and neither does it need as much fat and protein as normal. What the body does need, however, is carbohydrates. Choice of food is obviously personal, but it is important to have food you know you like to eat. Most people experience an extremely reduced desire to eat at high altitudes, which makes it difficult to meet the increased caloric intake required for strenuous exertion.

You also need to have food that can be cooked easily. Water boils at 87° C/189° F at the elevation of La Paz (3,600 m/11,800 ft) and at progressively lower temperatures the higher you go. From personal experience, this rules out rice (including so-called 10-minute rice). Eat as soon as possible after returning to camp. If you eat carbohydrates within 1 hour after exercising, your muscles will recover in the shortest possible time. If you don't eat within 3 hours, your muscles will begin to deteriorate.

Packaged foods, including soups, powdered drinks, noodles, biscuits, and chocolate, can be bought in La Paz from shops and stalls at the corner of Calle Isaac Tamayo and Calle Tumusla. Fresh food (and a lot of packaged food) can be bought at the main market at the corner of Calle Rodríguez and Calle Max Paredes. Ready-to-eat pasta meals and other North American luxuries can be bought at North American prices from La Paz's biggest supermarket, Ketal, which is on Avenida Ballivían at the corner of Calle 15 in the Calacoto district of the Zona Sur.

FUEL

Camping Gaz cannisters are available from a number of La Paz climbing agencies, including Condoriri. Epigas and Coleman gas cannisters are sometimes available; however, leaded gas only is available from gas stations. Kerosene is available from a limited number of places, as is paraffin. Methylated alcohol spirit *(alcohol potable)* is available from street stalls at the corner of Calle Sagárnaga and Calle Illampu in La Paz and in village shops all over the country. A rather worrying number of Bolivians drink it, and there have been reports of porters in the Sorata area drinking climbers' cooking supplies while carrying their packs. White gas *(gasolina blanca)* is occasionally available from Bolivian Journeys, Colibri, and Andean Summits, all on Calle Sagárnaga for US$5 per liter.

EQUIPMENT

A limited but growing amount of new equipment is on sale in La Paz, including ropes, crampons, rucksacks, fleece clothing, gas cannisters (Epigas and Camping Gaz), and headlamp batteries. Prices for imported items are high owing to transportation costs and import duty. For example, a battery for a headlamp runs US$10. Condoriri, Calle Sagárnaga 339, telephone 319369, offers the best selection. (Condoriri also has an

Ridge walking, Katantica Central, Cordillera Apolobamba

excellent repair service for all types of clothing and sewable kit, including zipper, strap, and buckle replacement.)

The alternative to purchasing new equipment is to buy secondhand gear from outgoing climbers with an airline weight problem. The best noticeboards for buying and selling (plus finding partners for climbing or transport) are in the Hotel Torino on Calle Socabaya, Hostal Austria on Calle Yanacocha, and the Club Andino on Calle México.

All specialist mountaineering agencies have some equipment available to rent. Colibri has the biggest selection, including boots, crampons, axes, harnesses, ice screws, snowstakes, karabiners, tents, cookers, and clothing. Plastic boots size U.S. 11/European 45 and above are difficult to find as are sizes under U.S. 7/European 38. See Appendix C for a suggested equipment list.

PHOTOGRAPHY

North American- and European-quality film and processing are available in La Paz—at similar or lower prices. All types of film are available, but check the sell-by dates. It is possible to have slides developed without having them mounted *(solo revelado)* for US$3, making them easy to take home and eliminating the risk of carrying exposed film.

Recommended film processors are the Agfa Center, Calle Loayza 250, and Foto Linares, Calle Loayza, three doors above the Agfa Center. Foto Linares is the best place for anything out of the ordinary, for example, slides to prints, black-and-white developing, and repairs. Ask for Señor Rolando Calla, who speaks English but is only at the shop in the mornings from 10:30 A.M. to 12:30 P.M.

Camera batteries can go flat very quickly at high altitudes—make sure you have spares. Lithium batteries are difficult to find in Bolivia and very expensive. Protect your film from extreme cold; it can split when being loaded or wound.

CLIMBING SEASON

The Bolivian climbing season extends through the dry southern winter from May through September, with the best and most stable weather from June through August. Snow conditions are better in the earlier part of the season, and harder routes, such as the West Face of Huayna Potosí or Cabeza de Condor Directisima, are in their best condition during May and June. After that, the snow turns to ice, crevasses open up, snow bridges collapse, and serac falls pose a greater threat on the harder, steeper routes.

In August there is often a windy period for a week or so when the Surazo comes in from Argentina. In September the peasants (*campesinos,* never Indios) mark the arrival of spring by setting fire to every piece of nonuseful vegetation they can lay their hands on. A number of explanations (that do not include land clearance) are given for this practice: A popularly held belief is that smoke creates clouds and clouds create rain, so burning vegetation must create rain. Also, some tough grasses are inedible for grazing animals, but fresh shoots are tender and tasty, so burning the grass promotes new growth for livestock. However, the land can recover only three times from this type of burning. Despite increasing efforts by the government to stop this custom, Illimani often cannot be seen from La Paz for much of September because of the smoke (*el humo*).

The weather becomes less predictable with more cloud cover during October and November before the rains start in December. The rainy season lasts until March or April, with storms nearly every day. The higher temperatures at this time of year (the southern summer) cause the snow to take on a porridgelike consistency, which makes it very hard to get anywhere and you can't see anything anyway.

This general pattern is upset for a week or two every five or so years when the increasingly studied El Niño (The Christ child) weather system causes devastation in coastal Ecuador and Peru and bad weather in Bolivia's mountains. In 1997 a team of U.S. scientists spent six weeks on the summit of Bolivia's highest mountain, Sajama, drilling ice cores up to 120 m/400 ft deep to study El Niño's impact over the last 20,000 years. The last El Niño was in 1997/98.

Being in the tropics, Bolivian nights are 11–12 hours long throughout the year.

GETTING TO THE PEAKS

How you get to the start of a route and how much support you want depends on your skills, finances, and preferences and the route you are attempting. An agency can organize everything, but if you want to go it alone, then do it yourself—it's invariably cheaper but requires more time.

Agencies and Guides

Many agencies in La Paz offer guides, transportation, cooks, porters, and camp guards—as much or as little as you want. English-, French- and German-speaking guides are sometimes available. If you are paying for a cook and food, ask to see the menu to make sure you like what you will be getting.

The Bolivian Mountain Guides Association has fewer than 30 members and is not yet recognized by the Union Internationale des Associations des Guides de Montagne (UIAGM). It does not include all mountain guides working in Bolivia—a number of Bolivia's better known and older guides are not in the association. Many guides who are not members of the association might have done the normal route many times but would be lost if they came off it and will have very little if any experience of bad weather or training in rescue methods.

The Club Andino Boliviano is basically a ski organization and runs the Chacaltaya ski lift and hut. It is based at Calle México 1638, Casilla 1346, telephone/fax Bolivia (+591) La Paz (2) 324682.

A number of specialist mountaineering agencies are located in La Paz:
Andean Summits, Calle Sagárnaga 189, Casilla 6976, telephone/fax 317497, e-mail: andean@latinwide.com—French and some English spoken.

Colibri, Calle Sagárnaga 309, Casilla 7456, telephone 371936, fax 323274, e-mail: acolibri@ceibo.entelnet.bo—Run by the very experienced Oscar Sainz, who speaks some English and is fluent in French.

EcoAdventure Andean and Amazon Expeditions, First Floor, Calle Illampu 738, Casilla 9434, telephone/fax 376776, e-mail: ecoadven@ceibo.entelnet.bo—Run by two young guides, Aldo Riveros and Tibeault Mesili, who speak some English and French.

Ozono, Calle Pedro Salazar 2485, Casilla 5258, telephone 323101, fax 433202, e-mail: yossibrain@hotmail.com—Completely English speaking, run by British-born, La Paz-based guide Yossi Brain; also German and French speakers.

TAWA, Calle Sagárnaga 161, Casilla 8662, telephone 325796, fax 391175, e-mail: tawa@caoba.entelnet.bo—French and English speaking.

Public Transportation

It is possible to get within walking, mule, or llama distance of some of the mountains—but not all—by using public transportation (detailed information is included under each mountain).

Bolivian public transportation outside the cities is normally in the back of a truck *(camión),* which is cheap but slow and incredibly dirty. Bigger towns and villages are linked to La Paz by regular bus services at various intervals, from hourly to weekly. Buses are slow, and you will find the ride uncomfortable if you are taller than 172 cm/5 ft 8 in because you will spend the journey smashing your kneecaps into the back of the seat in front of you.

Crampon and ice ax protectors are necessary if you use public transportation, during which these items should be packed inside your sack. Rice/flour/sugar sacks are available from markets and make ideal rucksack protectors. Covered up in this way, your sack will look just like any other piece of luggage and not a gringo sack worth stealing.

Drivers

Four-wheel drive vehicles with up to nine seats are the standard vehicles for getting to the mountains in Bolivia. A large roof rack is used to carry all the kit. These vehicles are usually driver-owned.

A number of very good, experienced, and reliable drivers are available, but many others will offer to drive you to a destination without

Jeep stop on the way back from Illimani, Cordillera Real

actually knowing where it is and then, not surprisingly, get lost. Booking through a reputable agency means you will get a decent driver and backup in case of breakdowns, accidents, and so forth. Drivers, like guides, are not legally allowed to work independently. Prices vary slightly among agencies.

Porters and Pack Animals

Porters are readily available for trips to the high camps on Illimani, Ancohuma, Illampu, and Sajama, and by arrangement elsewhere. Standard pay is US$10 per day. If there is any possibility that the porters will have to cross snow, ensure that they have crampons and sunglasses. As the employer, you are responsible for their well-being.

Mules can carry 40 kg/88 lbs each, and anyone who tells you differently is ripping you off.

Llamas can carry more than 20 kg/44 lbs, except the especially weak llamas of Cocoyo, which, for reasons having nothing to do with the llamas and a lot to do with their owners, can carry only 12 kg/26 lbs each.

Except at Condoriri and Illimani (or in cases where trips have been prearranged), muleteers *(arrieros)* normally have to go and get the animals, which might be kept in fields 3 or 4 hours away from the village or starting point.

For a 1-day trip using pack animals or porters, it is normal to agree on a price beforehand and then pay in full at the end of the day. For longer trips, arrangements are a bit more complicated. After agreeing on a price, pay a deposit of no more than 25 percent. Pay the remainder of the fee upon arrival at the destination. Do not submit to any requests for payment during the trip. Sometimes the *arrieros* decide they have had enough, and if you have paid them what they are owed, they will leave. If they do decide to go early, there is no reason to pay them any more than the deposit you have already paid. Just tell them you will pay at the end of the journey as agreed upon.

Although Bolivian guides are expected to have their own equipment, *arrieros* are not. This means, especially in the Apolobamba, that the *arrieros* will need tents, stoves, and food.

A written contract is a good way to make obligations and commitments clear to everyone. See Appendix D for a sample contract.

Security

The use of camp guards is growing among climbers in Bolivia. Porters and others will offer themselves as camp guards whenever you go to a popular mountain, especially Condoriri, Illimani, and Ancohuma-Illampu. The cost for each guard is around US$4 per day per group. However, camp guards are not a 100 percent guarantee of security because sometimes they are bribed to "look the other way." An alternative is to use your porter and muleteer as guards because they have a vested interest in your kit being there for them to carry back. As of this writing, there does not appear to be a protection racket running. For example, if you decline to use a camp guard, it is not certain that you will be robbed.

During June 1997 there was a short-lived theft problem from tents at the Illimani Puente Roto base camp. Remember that all your gear should be inside your tent; inside the vestibule is not good enough. There was a major problem with kit being stolen from tents in the Zongo Pass area below Huayna Potosí. It now appears to be safe to camp behind the dam guardian's house; alternatively, stay at the pass or the refuge, or camp in the valley below Charquini (see Huayna Potosí approach map).

If anything is stolen or if you have any other serious problems, report them to the tourist police in La Paz, located next to Disco Love City opposite the Hernando Siles soccer stadium in Miraflores (telephone 225016). If you are robbed, you will not see your kit again, but you will need a police report for insurance. If the police are made aware of a specific problem, they will take action.

MAPS

The Bolivian Instituto Geográfico Militar (IGM) produces 1:50,000 scale maps of much of the country, excluding some border areas and the Cordillera Apolobamba. Because of glacial retreat, the blue ice contours on the maps exaggerate the area of permanent snow and ice cover. Names are often wrong on the IGM maps, and many roads are missing, unless the maps are recent updates.

Maps are available with 24-hours notice from the IGM sales office, Oficina 5, at Calle Juan XXIII 100, a mud track behind the central post office off Calle Rodríguez between Calle Murillo and Calle Linares. The office is open Monday through Friday from 8:30 A.M. to 12:00 P.M. and from 2:30 P.M. to 6:00 P.M. If you want maps immediately, go to the IGM Headquarters, Estado Mayor, Avenida Bautista Saavedra, Miraflores, Monday through Friday from 9:00 A.M. to 11:00 A.M. and from 3:00 P.M. to 5:00 P.M. Take your passport with you because you will be on a military base. If the original color map (US$7) is not available, the IGM will provide a black-and-white photocopy (US$5.50) of limited use.

A New Map of the Cordillera Real, first published in 1996 (second edition, 1998) by Liam O'Brien, is an excellent 1:150,000 scale map to use for planning trips in the Cordillera Real because it shows all the road accesses. (Although not all the roads shown in the area to the west of Chachacomani and Chearoco are passable.) It is available in La Paz for US$10 from various outlets and also available direct from Liam O'Brien, 28 Turner Terrace, Newtonville, MA 02160, U.S.A.

Walter Guzmán Córdova produces 1:50,000 scale maps on glossy tear-resistant paper for Condoriri-Negruni, Huayna Potosí, Mururata-Illimani, Ancohuma-Illampu, and Sajama, which are available from Los Amigos del Libro, Calle Mercado 1315. These maps are based on the IGM maps, and once again, names are not always correct.

The German Alpine Club (Deutscher Alpenverein) produces two excellent 1:50,000 scale maps, one of Illimani and the other of Ancohuma-Illampu, which are available from the IGM sales office and sometimes from Los Amigos del Libro.

Outside Bolivia, some maps are available in the United States from

Omni Resources, 1004 South Mebane Street, P.O. Box 2096, Burlington, NC 27216, telephone 910 227-8300, fax 910 227-3740; and from Maplink, 25 East Mason Street, Dept G, Santa Barbara, CA 93101, telephone 805 965-4402; and in the United Kingdom from Stanfords, 12–14 Long Acre, London WC2E 9LP, telephone 0171 836-1321, fax 0171 836-0189.

Ozono (see the section "Agencies and Guides") can supply any map available in Bolivia.

ALTITUDE ILLNESS

Two forms of altitude illness, High Altitude Pulmonary Edema (HAPE) and High Altitude Cerebral Edema (HACE), are life-threatening illnesses. The treatment for both is *immediate* descent to a lower elevation. Once symptoms appear, victims deteriorate rapidly, so immediate descent is essential.

Mountains in Bolivia, as in many other parts of the world, are climbed following the adage "Climb high, sleep low." This way of climbing is based on an initial but far from complete period of acclimatization followed by swift climbs, getting up and down as fast as possible. The standard altitude advice of climbing 300 m/1,000 ft per day and having a rest day every third day when above 3,000 m/10,000 ft is the recommended rate of ascent to acclimatize. However, Bolivian mountains are successfully climbed by climbers on short holidays (for example, 2 weeks) who do not fully acclimatize. If you wanted to acclimatize as you went up, it would take 3 days to get from La Paz's southern suburbs to the city's airport, a journey normally done in 45 minutes.

In general, climbers visiting Bolivia appear to be ready to climb above 5,000 m/16,000 ft after 5 to 7 days at the height of La Paz or equivalent. However, climbers on short trips to Bolivia should not attempt itineraries sometimes done by climbers living in La Paz, such as Huayna Potosí in 24 hours or Illimani in 2 days. A person not fully acclimatized to the height of La Paz would at best feel ill and at worst die of HAPE or HACE.

High Altitude Pulmonary Edema (HAPE). This condition occurs when the blood-gas barrier in the lungs starts breaking up owing to the difference in pressure between the pulmonary artery and the air inside the lungs. If untreated, the victim will drown. Symptoms include the need to sit upright in order to breathe, pink frothy sputum, blue lips, severe breathlessness, and gargling in the lungs. Treatment is immediate descent and nefedepine.

High Altitude Cerebral Edema (HACE). This condition is caused by the brain swelling up and pressing against the skull. If untreated, HACE leads to brain hemorrhage, coma, and death. Symptoms include a severe headache, vomiting, loss of balance, disorientation, vision problems, incoherent speech, behavioral changes, and ultimately coma. Treatment is immediate descent and dexamethasone (Decadron). Dexamethasone is a steroid that works directly to reduce the size of the brain. If the victim experiences a debilitating headache, administer four 2mg pills immediately, followed by one pill four times a day while descending to a lower altitude. If the victim is in a coma, inject 8mg dexamethasone phosphate immediately in the upper outer quadrant of the buttock and descend. Inject another 4mg every 6 hours.

SLEEP DISTURBANCE

A common occurrence during sleep at high altitude is periodic (Cheyne-Stokes) breathing, a condition in which the sleeper stops breathing every cycle. At sea level, this is a serious problem, and it will get you sent to a hospital. At high altitudes, it is a common condition that causes worry for tent mates who initially think that the other person has died. The quality of sleep at high altitude is poor, with more arousals and less rapid eye movement (REM) sleep. The arousals lead to a person waking up while in the middle of a dream; hence, dreams often appear more vivid than at sea level.

SUN PROTECTION

Ultraviolet (UV) light at high altitude is very, very strong. Without proper eye protection, it is possible to get snow blindness after as little as 15 minutes above 5,000 m/16,000 ft. It does not matter if it is sunny or cloudy, in fact more UV light is reflected on cloudy days. Snow blindness is not normally apparent until the night after the damage has been done. The pain has been described as an excruciating burning sensation. The next day, the victim often cannot see and will have to be led down the mountain. Amethocaine eye drops help relieve the pain. Snow blindness causes permanent eye injury—part of the retina is burnt out—so victims are more susceptible in the future. Wear sunglasses that give 100 percent protection against UV light. Ski goggles with 100 percent UV protection lenses are useful for cloudy days, bad weather, and as spares in case you break or lose your glacier glasses.

Summiting Jankho Laya in a dry year, with Chachacomani in the background, Cordillera Real

Sunburn is a serious business at high altitude and will happen on completely overcast days. The best protection is to keep all your skin covered—a hat or helmet is essential to avoid sunstroke, a face mask is better than any suntan lotion or block, and a noseguard that clips to your sunglasses prevents getting suntan lotion all over your glasses. If you use sunblock, it should be zinc oxide-based.

FOOD POISONING AND GIARDIA

After acclimatization, the most common mountain health problem is suffering from a case of food poisoning picked up in La Paz. A course of antibiotics such as ciprofloxacin and oral rehydration salts generally takes effect quickly and allows ascent to continue.

It is possible to contract giardia anywhere there are animals, and llamas are quite happy up to 5,000 m/16,000 ft. The main indicator of giardia is diarrhea together with a huge and painful buildup of gas in the stomach and intestines and "farting through your mouth." Use iodine-based water purification tablets or tincture or a two-stage filter pump to treat all water while you are out climbing. Tincture of iodine works better than pills in the cold, and 30 ml bottles can be bought from pharmacies in La Paz (ask for *"iodo"*). If you get giardia, take tinidazole or metronidazole antibiotics.

ACCIDENTS

No formal rescue service or arrangements are available in Bolivia, so if you or a member of your party has an accident, you're on your own. Transportation is so poor that by the time anyone gets to you who isn't already on the mountain, it's probably going to be too late. There are only a few helicopters in the country, and they do not fly above 5,000 m/ 16,000 ft. If you can get access to a telephone, call your embassy or consulate. Insurance is expensive, but it is essential for air-evacuation home. Medical care is limited in Bolivia, and any serious injuries should be treated in North America or Europe.

This much said, serious accidents are rare in part because of the consistently stable and good weather during the climbing season. Ten fatalities occurred from 1994 through 1998. Solo climbers should carry their passports with them so that identification is possible should a tragedy occur.

The following hospitals are the best in La Paz:

Clinica Alemana, Avenida 6 de Agosto 2821, telephone 430355.

Clinica del Sur, Avenida Hernando Siles 5353, Obrajes, telephone 784750.

ENVIRONMENTAL IMPACT

Mountaineering has, so far, had little environmental impact in Bolivia mainly because only limited numbers of climbers visit the country. Outside the normal routes on Huayna Potosí and Illimani and at Condoriri base camp, it is normally possible to walk in, camp, and climb without seeing any other parties or signs of previous parties. However, the more people who climb in Bolivia, the more care that will have to be taken to maintain the mountains in their near-pristine condition.

All trash must be carried out to La Paz, where there is the closest attempt at decent rubbish disposal. If you can carry your packets, tins, and other rubbish up the mountain, there is no reason why you can't carry them down. Do not put your trash in a separate bag and give it to porters to carry down because they will throw it down the nearest crevasse or behind the nearest rock. Pack your trash into a rucksack. Do not leave your trash at the village at the bottom of the mountain—it will be thrown in the river. Burn toilet paper, and bury feces.

Bolivians do not regard litter as a problem beyond being something that is no longer wanted in their immediate personal space, be it pocket, car, bus, or house. Litter is dropped, thrown out of vehicle windows, and dumped outside houses. If you give a porter a boiled sweet or bar of chocolate, he or she will immediately throw the wrapper away, wherever he or she might be. So if you employ porters or other Bolivians, you must take responsibility for their litter as well. If you give them sweets, ask for the wrappers back.

HOW TO USE THIS BOOK

The mountains are grouped by cordillera in the following order: Apolobamba, Real, Quimsa Cruz, and Occidental. Geologically, the Apolobamba (to the north), Real, and Quimsa Cruz (to the south) are the same range. The Occidental is geologically and geographically distinct, lying to the west of the Altiplano.

For each of the four cordilleras, a brief overall description is followed by information on access and available maps. A map of the cordillera shows the locations of the mountains described.

All mountains are listed from north to south. Where appropriate, access, approach, and routes are grouped into different sets, for example, East Face and West Face, North Peak and South Peak.

The approach route is shown on a map for each mountain, and the maps that are available are listed. Topo photographs with route lines marked are included where available. For each mountain and route described, the following information is given.

Alternative names. Where relevant, alternative names are given in parentheses after the most commonly used name for the mountain. These might be found in older descriptions of mountaineering in Bolivia. For example, IGM maps are covered in mountains called "Cerro Illampu" and "Cerro Condoriri," whereas today's climbers recognize only one Illampu and one Condoriri. IGM maps sometimes give completely unused names as well. The O'Brien map uses the current standard Aymara spelling of mountain names, which is often confusing, for example, "Ancohuma" becomes "Janq'uma." Peasants living in the mountain localities often use completely different names than those used by map makers and climbers. Spelling of names varies, but common alternative spellings of any word include the following variations: The hard "c" sound, as in "crampon," can be spelled with "c" or "k." The "kh" combination, as in "khota," is often spelled "kkota" or "quta." The letters "q" and "k" also appear interchangeably. Currently "k" is preferred over "q," so for example, "Taquesi" becomes "Takesi."

Heights. Writing in the *American Alpine Journal* (1943–45), Josef Prem stated: "What one finds in the schoolbooks and almanacs about the altitude of Bolivian mountains is pure fancy." Considerable differences in stated heights for Bolivian mountains still exist, with the most obvious being Ancohuma, which is regularly listed as 7,010 m/22,998 ft rather than the generally accepted 6,427 m/21,086 ft. Heights listed here are the most accurate known and come from a variety of sources.

To convert meters to feet, multiply by 3.2808. (Or for a reasonably accurate estimate, multiply by 3 and add 10 percent.) To convert feet to meters, divide by 3.2808.

First known/recorded ascent of mountain and/or route. The most complete information possible is given—ideally the month, day, and year of the ascent and the first and last names and the nationalities of the first ascensionists in alphabetical order. Omissions are owing to a lack of information, and any additional information will be gratefully received and acknowledged in future editions.

Maps. The best available map is given first, followed by alternative maps in case the best map is no longer available. If two or more IGM maps are listed, it means two or more maps are needed to cover the mountain.

Access. The best route by public and private transportation to base camp is described, as well as any other relevant options. Note: Public transportation arrangements change regularly to take into account public holidays (national, regional, and local), elections, and sometimes soccer matches. Always check before you travel.

Approach. The best walk-in approach to base camps and/or high camps is described.

Routes. For each major peak, a selection of routes is described. However, the exact line of a route changes from season to season and even during a season as crevasses open and close.

Grade. Two sets of grades are given for each climb: one for North American readers, the other for Europeans.

The first grade is a U.S. alpine grade for snow/ice routes with a Yosemite Decimal System grade in brackets for rock pitches when relevant. The second grade is a French alpine grade followed by a Union Internationale des Associations d'Alpinisme rock grade in brackets when relevant.

The U.S. system is based on the Welzenbach scale, which rates routes from Grade I to Grade VI, with Grade I used for routes up to 50° snow or 35° ice and gets progressively harder until Grade VI, which is used for routes with very thin or technical 90° ice.

The French alpine system is similar, but it uses words abbreviated to letters instead of numerals. It starts at F for *Facile* (easy) and proceeds through PD (*Peu Difficile*—a little difficult), AD (*Assez Difficile*—fairly difficult), D (*Difficile*—difficult), TD (*Très Difficile*—very difficult), and ED (*Extrêmement Difficile*—extremely difficult).

The overall grade of the route takes into consideration technical difficulty, the difficulty of the hardest section of the route, exposure, commitment, and so forth. However, because all the routes start at over 5,000 m/16,000 ft, acclimatization is as important as technical ability. There is always more snow at the start of the season, with more icy sections at the end of the season. Plowing through unconsolidated snow at high altitudes obviously takes more time. Névé snow is a delight; ice makes climbing harder.

Maximum slope. The approximate angle of the steepest section of the route is given. This is steeper than the average slope of the route, but it shows the maximum difficulty.

Elevation gain. Vertical altitude gain is estimated from the logical start of the route where the climbing begins. This is often from the bergschrund, but normally lower, from the start of the glacier or from the base camp or high camp.

Time required. This is an approximate timing based on a fit and acclimatized rope climbing in good to average conditions.

cordillera apolobamba

. . . the Venusian world of ice, of sudden reckless mists of palpable

water, of lichen and trickling springs, of fragmenting shale and

glistening white peaks, where human realities become remote and

ridiculous, where the sky is actually below you and inside you, where

breathing is an accomplishment in itself, and where condors,

inconceivably ponderous and gigantic, wheel on the upcurrents like

lords of a different and fantastic universe.

Louis de Bernières
The War of Don Emmanuel's Nether Parts, 1990

he rarely visited Cordillera Apolobamba is to the north of Lake Titicaca and crosses the border into Peru. The cordillera was un-visited by any mountaineering expedition until 1957, and there are still unclimbed peaks over 5,000 m/16,000 ft. Geologically, the cordillera is the northern extension of the main Cordillera Real, and the climb-ing is similar, although lower, with most peaks in the 5,500 m/18,000 ft

In the southeast couloir of Cololo, Cordillera Apolobamba

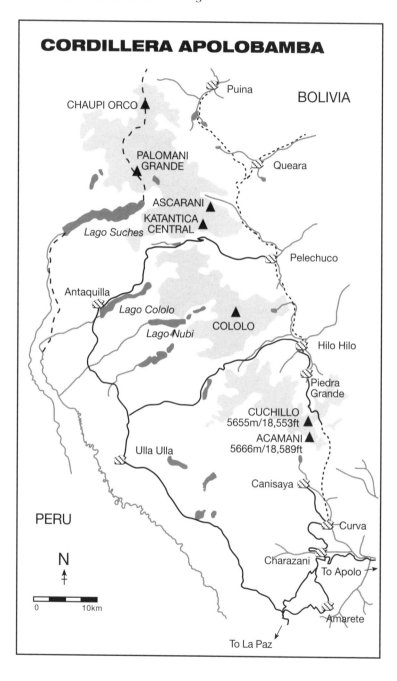

CORDILLERA APOLOBAMBA

Puina

BOLIVIA

CHAUPI ORCO ▲

PALOMANI
GRANDE ▲

Queara

ASCARANI ▲
KATANTICA ▲
Lago Suches CENTRAL

Pelechuco

Antaquilla

Lago Cololo

Lago Nubi

COLOLO ▲

Hilo Hilo

Piedra
Grande

CUCHILLO ▲
5655m/18,553ft

ACAMANI ▲
5666m/18,589ft

Ulla Ulla

Canisaya

PERU

Curva

Charazani

To Apolo

N
↑

0   10km

Amarete

To La Paz

range. Literally thousands of new routes remain to be climbed, but the difficulty in getting to the region and the lack of maps appear to have dissuaded climbers—or anyone else for that matter—from going there.

The peaks of the Cordillera Apolobamba are listed north to south and are divided into the Northern Apolobamba and the Southern Apolobamba with the division at the Pelechuco valley.

For the Northern Apolobamba, access is via the village of Pelechuco. For mountains in the south, go in via the villages of Charazani and Curva, though Cololo is accessed from Pelechuco or the Altiplano.

ACCESS VIA PELECHUCO

Pelechuco is situated at 3,600 m/11,800 ft. The village has a medical post, normally staffed, a number of shops that sell the basics, and a number of eateries where set meals cost US$1–1.60. Accommodations are basic and cheap at US$1–1.50 per person per night. The best place to stay is the grandly named Hotel Llajtaymanta, a small *alojamiento* (lodging) attached to the restaurant opposite the church. The village has electricity intermittently, water comes from taps in the streets, and sanitation is extremely basic. Fiestas take place every month in Pelechuco with the largest on and around July 25, the village's founding date, when it is extremely difficult to find anyone sober enough to drive a mule.

The bus from La Paz to Pelechuco leaves from the corner of Calle Reyes Cardona and Avenida Kollasuyo, 3 blocks up from Cementerio, Wednesday at 8:00 A.M. The trip costs US$7 and takes 14–24 hours. The return bus from Pelechuco to La Paz leaves Friday and Saturday at 7:00 P.M., but check times before you go.

To or from Pelechuco by jeep costs up to US$400 and takes 10 hours. The journey through the Río Pelechuco valley is well worth doing in daylight. If you travel by jeep, a visit to the thermal baths 2 hours outside of Pelechuco, near Antaquilla, is a must, followed by a trip through the Reserva Nacional de Fauna Ulla Ulla to spot vicuña.

Mules can be hired in Pelechuco.

ACCESS VIA CHARAZANI

Charazani (official name Villa Juan J. Perez) is the biggest village in the Apolobamba region. At 3,200 m/10,500 ft, it is noticeably warmer than La Paz, and the thermal baths 10 minutes below the village are a great place in which to unwind (entrance US$1). Small shops and eateries are found around the square as well as a number of *alojamientos,* the best being Hotel Akhamani, with rooms for US$1.40–2 per person per night. Trout is often available for the set evening meal. The village has a medical post, but no telephone, and there has not been any electricity since 1994. A big fiesta occurs around July 16.

ACCESS VIA CURVA

Curva is an attractive hilltop village at 3,900 m/12,800 ft. It is the capital village of the Kallawayas, traveling witch doctors of the area, and is situated below their sacred mountain of Acamani. However, Curva has nothing to offer visitors in terms of accommodations or food. Its fiesta is particularly well supported by the local population for most of the week around June 29. Mules are available for hire here.

Buses from La Paz to Charazani depart daily at 6:00 A.M. They leave from the same place as the buses to Pelechuco, the corner of Calle Reyes Cardona and Avenida Kollasuyo, above Cementerio. The trip costs US$4.40 and takes 10 hours. The Charazani bus sometimes goes all the way to Curva if enough passengers want to continue. The trip to Curva takes 1½ hours and costs US$1.40. The return bus to La Paz leaves Charazani daily at 7:00 P.M.

A jeep from La Paz to or from Curva costs up to US$300 and takes 8 hours (6½ hours to Charazani). Ask the driver to go via the village of Amarete, which is more reminiscent of Nepal than Bolivia. If you leave La Paz by jeep by 6:00 A.M., you should arrive in Curva (with stops) between 3:00 P.M. and 4:00 P.M.

Note: The Apolobamba is a border area, and you will pass through a series of military checkpoints. Take your passport with you.

MAPS

There are no maps of the Apolobamba published in Bolivia. The best available map is that done by the Boundary Commission of the Royal Geographic Society (RGS) in 1911–13, updated by Paul Hudson in 1993, and published by the RGS, London. The map has mistakes and omissions, but it is by far the best one available.

Ice formation on Ascarani with Chaupi Orco in the background, Cordillera Apolobamba

northern apolobamba

CHAUPI ORCO

6,044 m/19,829 ft

AUGUST 1, 1957, WERNER KARL, HANS RICHTER, AND HANS WIMMER (GERMANY)

The highest mountain in the Cordillera Apolobamba is called rather ungrandly in Quechua, "Middle Peak." Chaupi Orco's exact height is in dispute: the Peruvians who share the mountain with Bolivia say it is 5,999 m/19,682 ft, and the Russians claim it is 5,920 m/19,422 ft. Whatever the height, it dominates all high views north from within the cordillera. The approach is long, by Bolivian standards, but beautiful.

Approach

Travel from Pelechuco to base camp takes 2 days with mules. (Most muleteers will try to convince you it is a 3-day trip, but it isn't.) It takes 1 day to get up the glacier and 1 day to summit and return to base camp.

Day 1: With your back to the Pelechuco church, exit the square via the far right-hand corner, go down, and after a couple of minutes, cross the river next to the medical center. Follow the new dirt road down and

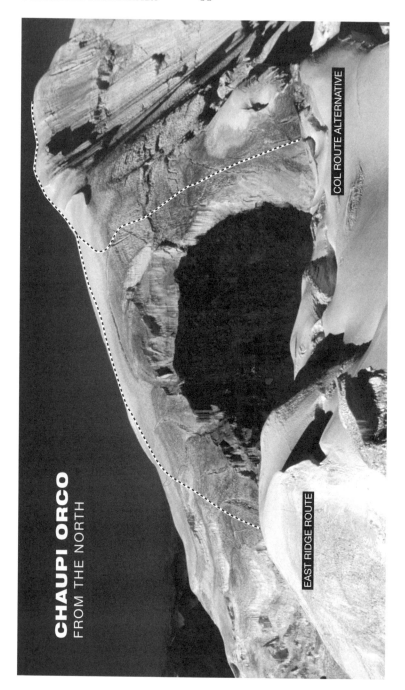

CHAUPI ORCO
FROM THE NORTH

COL ROUTE ALTERNATIVE

EAST RIDGE ROUTE

after 20 minutes follow the path up to the left, heading left into the valley of the Río Sanches Cuchu (also known as the Río Macara). Above the small village of Macara, cross a bridge to the right-hand side of the valley, and continue up to Paso Sánches at 4,840 m/15,880 ft. Stay on the left while crossing the broad pass area, and descend to camp near derelict farm buildings, 5½ hours from Pelechuco.

Day 2: Descend to the stream, cross it, and move up through Paso Yanacocha (4,760 m/15,620 ft). Descend on the other side, passing through a notch in the ridge, and then go down steep zigzags to a river. Climb up on the other side, staying on the left-hand side of the valley, and cross another pass. Descend to a lake, and then follow the exit stream until you arrive above the large and sedimented Lago Soral (4,120 m/13,520 ft). From here, drop diagonally down toward the left (top) end of Lago Soral, and then go up to and across a large boggy pampa. Base camp is at the far end (4,280 m/14,040 ft). A clear stream comes down into the far left corner of the pampa. To reach base camp takes 6½ hours with mules from the previous night's camp.

Day 3: From base camp, head up the path on the left-hand side of the obvious moraine ridge. When you reach the top of the moraine, head up and left—do not drop down to the glacier, which is very broken and difficult to cross. Follow a faint path marked by occasional cairns to reach a moraine ridge that divides two glaciers. Walk along the ridge until near its end, where you drop down to the right. Plod up the glacier as far as you can get, aiming for the flat far end (5,200 m/17,060 ft), which takes 5–7 hours from base camp.

EAST RIDGE ROUTE

Grade II/AD, 45°, 850 m/2,800 ft, 6 hours

From camp on the glacier due east of Chaupi Orco, head through the crevasse field to join the ridge on its northern side at the base of the easiest slopes up. Move up on to the ridge, and then follow it over a series of false summits to the true summit.

An alternative way up or down is to head up the left-hand side of the glacier coming down from the col immediately north of Chaupi Orco. At the col, turn left, and move up more directly to the ridge. At the ridge, turn right, and continue to the summit.

Descent: Same

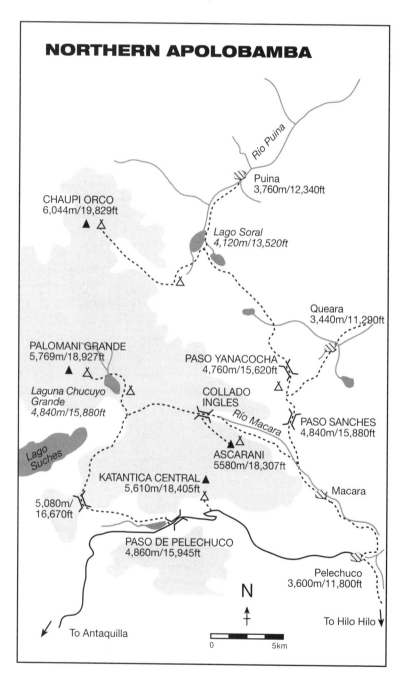

NORTHERN APOLOBAMBA

Río Puina

Puina
3,760m/12,340ft

CHAUPI ORCO
6,044m/19,829ft

Lago Soral
4,120m/13,520ft

Queara
3,440m/11,290ft

PALOMANI GRANDE
5,769m/18,927ft

PASO YANACOCHA
4,760m/15,620ft

Laguna Chucuyo
Grande
4,840m/15,880ft

COLLADO
INGLES

Río Macara

PASO SANCHES
4,840m/15,880ft

Lago
Suches

ASCARANI
5580m/18,307ft

KATANTICA CENTRAL
5,610m/18,405ft

Macara

5,080m/
16,670ft

PASO DE PELECHUCO
4,860m/15,945ft

Pelechuco
3,600m/11,800ft

N

To Hilo Hilo

To Antaquilla

0   5km

SOUTHWEST RIDGE ROUTE

JUNE 22, 1980, NICO BIDESE AND GIUSEPPE PIERANTONI (ITALY)

This route is long but not difficult. From the base camp above Lago Soral, cross the Southwest Ridge to set up a high camp to the west of the mountain. From the high camp, join the ridge, and follow it to the summit.

Descent: Same

PALOMANI GRANDE

5,769 m/18,927 ft

JUNE 28, 1958, ROMANO MERENDI, GIANLUIGI STERNA,
CAMILLO ZAMBONI (ITALY) FROM PERU

Palomani Grande is on the Bolivia-Peru border and is rarely climbed from the Bolivian side, although there are unsubstantiated claims that a Bolivian army captain climbed the mountain before 1932. The literal translation of the name is "Place of doves," for which there is no evidence either.

Approach via Paso de Pelechuco (also called Paso Katantica)

Travel to the pass from Pelechuco takes 2 hours by bus or jeep. Buses leave for the trip to La Paz from the square in Pelechuco Friday and Saturday at 7:00 P.M. (and often to a country market on the Altiplano on Thursday at 4:00 A.M.) and will take you to the pass for US$2. Alternatively, get off the La Paz-Pelechuco bus when it reaches the pass, about 1 hour from Antaquilla. A jeep takes 8 hours from La Paz and costs up to US$400. (The pass is the highest point of the road after it climbs out of Antaquilla, where there is a military checkpoint.)

From the pass, head down west, go around the first of two lakes, and then proceed into a valley heading north. It is possible to camp in this valley that leads up to a pass at 5,800 m/16,670 ft. If you have time, continue up and over the pass and descend on the other side before heading north to Laguna Chucuyo Grande, where it is possible to camp on the southeastern shore.

Palomani Grande can be climbed from Laguna Chucuyo Grande in 1 day, but an excellent high camp 2½ hours beyond the lake puts you only 45 minutes from the glacier. To reach the high camp, go around

PALOMANI GRANDE
FROM THE EAST

NORTH RIDGE ROUTE

EAST GULLY ROUTE

SOUTH RIDGE ROUTE

Laguna Chucuyo Grande, cross the stream which enters it from the north, and head up the valley beyond until you reach a stream coming down from the left. Follow this stream up. The high camp is in a grassy area near a clear lake (5,240 m/17,190 ft), which is also home to the often noisy Andean geese.

SOUTH RIDGE ROUTE

Grade II/AD, 60°, 250 m/800 ft, 1½ hours from high camp

MAY 5, 1996, TOTO ARAMAYO (BOLIVIA), DAVID BANDROWSKI (U.S.), YOSSI BRAIN (U.K.), AND ULLI SCHATZ (GERMANY)

To take this route, go up the right-hand side of the glacier to the ridge. Follow the ridge to the south summit, and then continue to the main summit. A short section of 60° is encountered along the way, but most of the route is 50° or less.

Descent: North Ridge Route

EAST GULLY ROUTE

Grade II/AD, 55°, 250 m/800 ft, 1½ hours

On this route, follow the gully from the bottom to the base of the summit ridge in between the south and the main summits. Turn right, and follow the ridge to the summit. Depending on snow conditions, there can be a short, steep step through a rock band one-third of the way up the gully.

Descent: North Ridge Route

NORTH RIDGE ROUTE

Grade II/AD-, 60°, 250 m/800 ft, 1½ hours

MAY 5, 1996, TOTO ARAMAYO (BOLIVIA), DAVID BANDROWSKI (U.S.), YOSSI BRAIN (U.K.), ULLI SCHATZ (GERMANY) DESCENDING

To take this route, go up the left-hand side of the glacier to the ridge—watch out for crevasses—and then go left to the main summit. Finish by climbing up the convex snow dome, which is the steepest part of the route.

Descent: Same

ASCARANI
(AZUCARANI)

5,580 m/18,307 ft

JULY 24, 1959, GEOFFREY BRATT, JOHN JENKINSON, WILLIAM MELBOURNE,
AND ARTHUR SMITH (U.K.)

A Spanish expedition in 1969 made 19 first ascents in the area north of Pelechuco and described Ascarani (where they made the second ascent) as the most beautiful peak they climbed. From base camp, it is a rock needle, but once you are on the glacier, it becomes an ice peak. Geoffrey Bratt, writing in the *American Alpine Journal* (1960–61), said: "delightful climbing on steep ice ridges and faces," which is as good a description as any.

Approach

Travel from Pelechuco to base camp takes 1 day. With your back to the Pelechuco church, exit the square via the far right-hand corner, go down, and after a couple of minutes, cross the river next to the medical center. Follow the new dirt road down and after 20 minutes follow the path up to the left, heading left into the valley. Above the village of Macara, cross a bridge to the right-hand side of the valley. When the path starts to climb up to the right, leave it to join a broad flat pampa at the end of the Río Macara valley (known locally as Chocoyo). Stay to the right of the stream until you are nearly below the obvious rock peak of Ascarani, and then cross to the left. Continue up to establish base camp in the last flat part of the valley (4,500 m/14,760 ft), 5 hours with mules from Pelechuco. The main stream is sedimented, but a number of small clear streams come down from the left.

From base camp, Ascarani has been accessed directly from the valley, which involves rock scrambling, a rappel, and a pretty tortuous route that takes 4 hours (5.4/III). Keep to the left of all the rock towers to reach the glacier to the right of the final tower. It is quicker to go via the Collado Inglés ("English Col") at the head of the Río Macara valley. Follow cow paths up to and along the moraine ridge to reach the col (5,160 m/16,930 ft). Go left, and continue over the rock until you can see the Northwest Ridge. For the Southwest Face, cross the glacier until you are directly below the face.

It is also possible to access Ascarani from the west via Paso de Pelechuco and Laguna Chucuyo Grande, and then cross the glacier to reach the base of the mountain. See the description for Palomani Grande above.

67

ASCARANI

ASCARANI
FROM THE WEST

NORTHWEST RIDGE ROUTE

SOUTHWEST FACE ROUTE

Topping out on the West Face of Ascarani, Cordillera Apolobamba
(Photo by Jason Currie)

NORTHWEST RIDGE ROUTE

Grade II/AD-, 50°, 300 m/1,000 ft, 2 hours from the Collado Inglés

JULY 24, 1959, GEOFFREY BRATT, JOHN JENKINSON, WILLIAM MELBOURNE,
AND ARTHUR SMITH (U.K.)

This route follows a beautiful and straightforward line, which averages 40°. Follow the ridge the whole way to the summit, staying on the snow.

Descent: Same

SOUTHWEST FACE ROUTE

Grade III/D, 55°, 300 m/1,000 ft, 1 hour from the bergschrund

JULY 18, 1996, JASON CURRIE AND MARK RYLE (U.K.)

This route is steeper than the Northwest Ridge, but it is just as beautiful. Cross the bergschrund toward the left-hand side, and then follow the uniform névé straight up to the summit.

Descent: Northwest Ridge Route

KATANTICA CENTRAL
(KATANTICA III)

5,610 m/18,405 ft

MAY 27, 1968, KARL GROSS AND DIETER HAIN (GERMANY) FROM THE EAST-NORTHEAST

The Katantica Group is made up of five peaks, three of which are in a west–east line (Katanticas Oeste, Central, and Este), with one to the southwest (Point 5550) and one to the southeast (Katantica Sur). The most obvious peak is Katantica Este, which has a long, almost horizontal, west shoulder leading up to the summit pyramid. Katantica Central (the next peak west) provides the most interesting climbing of the group.

Approach and Access

Start from the Pelechuco road due south of Katantica Este. Camping is possible on the other side of the stream from the road (4,400 m/14,440 ft), or continue up, following a moraine ridge that brings you to the glacier. Carry on up the glacier, heading left and staying to the northeast of Point 5550 to reach the col between Point 5550 and Katantica Central for a fantastic view of the West Ridge. A sheltered camping spot is found on the other side of the col.

KATANTICA CENTRAL
FROM THE COL BETWEEN POINT 5550
AND KATANTICA CENTRAL

WEST RIDGE ROUTE

Climbing Katantica Central, Cordillera Apolobamba
(Photo by Eamonn Flood)

WEST RIDGE ROUTE

Grade III/AD+, 65°, 400 m/1,300 ft, 4 hours

MAY 25, 1997, YOSSI BRAIN, EAMONN FLOOD, AND DEAN WIGGIN (U.K.)

This route follows a beautiful line, and it is probably the best route in the group. From the col between Point 5550 and Katantica Central, follow the West Ridge to the summit. The cornice switches from right to left—be careful on the right (south) slope, which appears to be made up of bottomless powder at about 70°. The angle eases, and the route finishes as a ridge walk to the summit.

Descent: From the summit, continue along the ridge, and then drop down toward the right, looking for the East–Southeast Face (the route used by the Germans in 1968). The face is steep at the top for 40 m/130 ft, and then becomes an easy walk down to the col between Katanticas Central and Este.

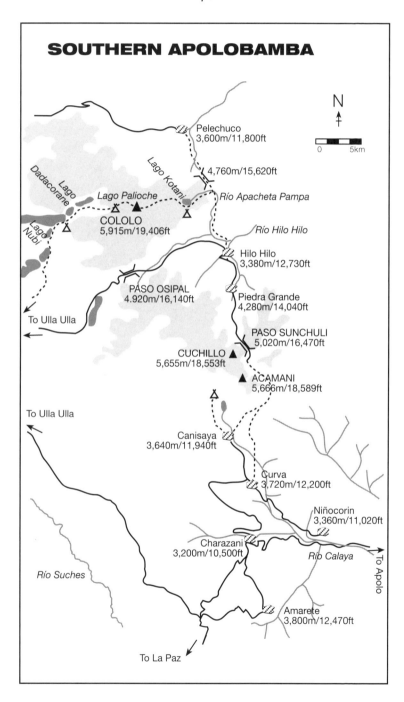

SOUTHERN APOLOBAMBA

N

0   5km

Pelechuco
3,600m/11,800ft

4,760m/15,620ft

Lago Kotani

Río Apacheta Pampa

Lago Dadacorane

Lago Palioche

COLOLO
5,915m/19,406ft

Lago Nubi

Río Hilo Hilo

Hilo Hilo
3,380m/12,730ft

PASO OSIPAL
4.920m/16,140ft

Piedra Grande
4,280m/14,040ft

To Ulla Ulla

PASO SUNCHULI
5,020m/16,470ft

CUCHILLO ▲
5,655m/18,553ft

▲ ACAMANI
5,666m/18,589ft

To Ulla Ulla

Canisaya
3,640m/11,940ft

Curva
3,720m/12,200ft

Niñocorin
3,360m/11,020ft

Charazani
3,200m/10,500ft

Río Calaya

To Apolo

Río Suches

Amarete
3,800m/12,470ft

To La Paz

Soloing up the west ridge of Cololo, Cordillera Apolobamba

southern apolobamba

COLOLO
(CCACHURA)

5,915 m/19,406 ft

JULY 23, 1957, WERNER KARL, HANS RICHTER, AND HANS WIMMER (GERMANY)

The second highest mountain in the Apolobamba is very visible from the Altiplano as a striking pyramid. The first ascent followed a peculiarly spiral route of the south face, east ridge, north face, west ridge, and

COLOLO
FROM THE COL
TO THE NORTHWEST

WEST RIDGE ROUTE

NORTH RIDGE ROUTE

finished up on the south face, which explains the 17-hour round trip the Germans needed to climb the mountain.

Approach

Traditionally, Cololo has been approached from the west via the end of Lago Nubi (4,600 m/15,090 ft), with climbers putting up a high camp on the glacier to the west of the mountain. However, it is easier to access the mountain via Pelechuco, especially if you are relying on public transportation to get to the Apolobamba. Travel to the base camp takes 1 day from the village with mules.

Facing Pelechuco church, leave the square by going up the cobbled street to the right of the church. After 30m/100 ft, the street makes a 90° left-hand turn. Continue along for a few minutes until you cross a stream. After the stream, immediately turn right and follow the path out of the village and on up to a pass in 4 hours (4,760 m/15,620 ft). Descend on the other side of the pass, and cross the stream. Immediately after the stream, turn right and follow animal paths up valley to reach an area locally known as Kotani. Lago Kotani (4,760 m/15,620 ft) is sediment-filled, but a clear stream runs into it from the top left, 6 hours from Pelechuco.

Cololo is easily recognizable from base camp above Lago Kotani. Head up valley, staying to the left of the stream and to the left of the moraine ridge until you join the glacier.

From this point, there are a number of options. You can go around the south (left) of the mountain up the Southeast Couloir, and then make your way across to the West Ridge. Alternatively, you can head for the snow section of the North Ridge, climb it, and then do the North Ridge, or you can descend on the other side, and head for the shoulder of the West Ridge.

WEST RIDGE ROUTE

Grade III+/D, 55°, 500 m/1,650 ft, 6 hours

AUGUST 9, 1988, DAVID HICK AND MICHAEL SMITH (U.K.)

This is the best route on the mountain. From the shoulder of the West Ridge, the last 200 m/650 ft of the route is impressively airy all the way to the summit.

Descent: Same or North Ridge Route

NORTH RIDGE ROUTE

Grade III/D-, 65°, 460 m/1,500 ft, 4 hours

AUGUST 9, 1989, PAMELA HOLT, DAVID TYSON, AND DAVID WOODCOCK (U.K.)

This route is an exercise in traversing multitowered loose rock. To reach the ridge, climb 65° snow from either the east or the west, and then follow the ridge to the summit. The final 200 m/650 ft is snow that might be corniced.

Descent: Same

SOUTHEAST RIDGE ROUTE

Grade III+/D-, 70°, 500 m/1,650 ft, 6 hours

JULY 21, 1986, BILL AND JAMES PETROSKE (U.S.)

To take this route, climb the west side of the ridge at 70° for 70 m/230 ft, and then cut on to the ridge proper and follow it to the summit. The ridge is exposed, with a 700 m/2,300 ft drop to the east.

Descent: North Ridge Route or West Ridge Route

CUCHILLO

5,655 m/18,553 ft

MAY 28, 1965, KEISUKE MIYAZAKI AND SHIGEYUKI OKAJIMA (JAPAN)

Cuchillo is a beautiful pyramid with ridiculously easy access—it is a roadside mountain. Another plus point for this peak is the quick and easy descent along the Northeast Ridge.

Approach

From the north: A jeep ride from La Paz to before the Paso Sunchuli takes 10 hours and costs up to US$400, or it's a 2-day trek from Curva in the south or Pelechuco to the north. From the village of Piedra Grande, follow the road up and out of the village. Immediately after crossing a stream, leave the road, and head up and left, following a path into a broad valley. You will rejoin the road later, staying on the right-hand side of the valley. After 2 hours, reach the top of this valley and camp.

From the south: Trek in from Curva, following the trail to Pelechuco and passing through Jatunpampa, Incachani, and Viscachani to reach the Sunchuli valley. Continue up and over the Paso Sunchuli to camp on the other side of the pass.

CUCHILLO
FROM THE NORTHEAST

SOUTHWEST RIDGE ROUTE

WEST FACE ROUTE

NORTHEAST RIDGE ROUTE

Descending the northeast ridge of Cuchillo, Cordillera Apolobamba

SOUTHWEST RIDGE ROUTE

Grade II/AD, 45°, 400m/1,300 ft, 2 hours

MAY 28, 1965, KEISUKE MIYAZAKI AND SHIGEYUKI OKAJIMA (JAPAN)

Climb up to join the ridge at the far (western) side of the West Face, and then follow it along to the summit.

Descent: Northeast Ridge Route (Grade I/PD). From the summit, walk down through easy *nieve penitentes* and then through scree to reach an old mining road that winds its way down to the Sunchuli road.

WEST FACE ROUTE

Grade II+/AD+, 50°, 400 m/1,300 ft, 2 hours

JULY 24, 1996, YOSSI BRAIN, JASON CURRIE, AND MARK RYLE (U.K.), SOLO

This route is a bit of a calf-burner. Join the glacier, and then work a way around and through it until you are directly below the face where the climbing starts. Head straight up to join the ridge slightly to the west of the summit. Snow conditions are normally excellent.

Descent: Northeast Ridge Route

ACAMANI

5,666 m/18,589 ft

AUGUST 10, 1961, KEI KURACHI, HIROSHI NAKAJIMA,

AND TAMOTSU NAKAMURA (JAPAN)

Acamani marks the southern end of the Cordillera Apolobamba and is sacred to the Kallawayas, the traveling medicine men of the area. While beautiful from afar, Acamani gets increasingly complicated the closer you get with the exception of the North Ridge, which is beautiful, straightforward, and by far the best line on the mountain.

Access and Approach

Hire a jeep for the trip from La Paz through Charazani to Curva. Just before you reach Curva, before the shallow lake, a road heads left up to a col, crosses it, and then continues to Canisaya, a beautiful stone and thatch village. A jeep costs US$350, and the journey takes 9 hours.

Buses to Charazani from La Paz leave from the corner of Calle Reyes Cardona and Avenida Kollasuyo above Cementerio daily at 6:00 A.M. (US$4.40, 10 hours). From Charazani, no regular public transportation is available to Curva or Canisaya, although the bus from La Paz to

ACAMANI
FROM SOUTHWEST

NORTH RIDGE

WEST FACE ROUTE

Charazani will sometimes continue to Curva if enough passengers want to go there. Walking takes 1 day from Charazani to Canisaya.

From the square in Canisaya, make your way to the river, cross it, and follow the path rising diagonally up to the left. Cross the pass, and contour along until you join the bottom of the next valley. Head up the valley through a series of fields *(pampas)* until you rise up and out of the last pampa. Set up base camp near the lake.

NORTH RIDGE ROUTE

Grade II (5.4)/AD (III), 50°, 300 m/1,000 ft, 3 hours
AUGUST 9–10, 1961, KEI KURACHI, HIROSHI NAKAJIMA,
AND TAMOTSU NAKAMURA (JAPAN)

This route is the most obvious and beautiful one on the mountain. Work your way across the glacier, avoiding the large crevasses, to reach the base of the short wall up to the ridge. Follow the ridge to the summit. The rock pitch is in reasonably good condition, but a piton and rappel speed up the descent.

Descent: Same

WEST FACE ROUTE

Grade III/AD+, 45–75°, 400 m/1,300 ft, 4 hours
JULY 27, 1996, YOSSI BRAIN, JASON CURRIE, AND MARK RYLE (U.K.), SOLO

This route is poor compared to the North Ridge, but it is a way to reach the south ridge. Pick a way through the glacier, avoiding the numerous large crevasses. Depending on the exact line, this can involve steep ice. When you reach the large snow ledge, follow it toward the right to the base of a number of gullies. Follow one of the ice gullies up to very loose rock and on to the col between the two rock buttresses and the upper part of the south ridge. Turn left, and continue to the summit.

Descent: North Ridge Route

cordillera real

Here is an unbroken chain of peaks and glaciers rising in a country

of much historic interest; for those who understand that height alone

does not mean everything there is practically no limit for mountain

adventure in the Cordillera Real.

Evelio Echevarría
American Alpine Journal, 1985

this world-class mountain range offers something for every climber, whatever his or her level of skill and experience. Because of its close proximity to La Paz, the Real is the most visited of Bolivia's ranges. However, outside the normal routes on Huayna Potosí, Illimani, and in the Condoriri Group, you can find routes and entire mountains to yourself with no sign of previous camps or climbs. Thousands of new routes remain to be climbed, especially on the eastern side of the cordillera where access is harder and the weather is worse. As Paul Drummond wrote in the *Alpine Journal* (1985), "The Real offers good enough climbing to satisfy most, although it is not easy to crack off new peaks—more because it is hard to find out about them and hard to get to them, rather than any real shortage of peaks."

Ice formations below Campamento Argentino, Huayna Potosí, Cordillera Real

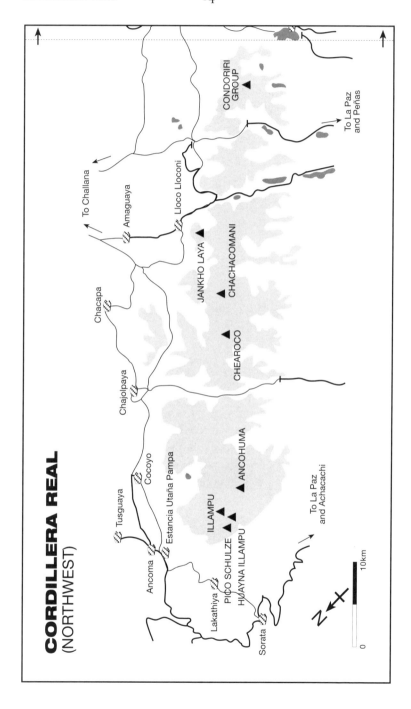

CORDILLERA REAL
(NORTHWEST)

To Challana

Amaguaya

Lloco Lloconi

CONDORIRI GROUP

To La Paz and Peñas

JANKHO LAYA

CHACHACOMANI

Chacapa

CHEAROCO

Chajolpaya

ANCOHUMA

Cocoyo

Estancia Utaña Pampa

Tusguaya

ILLAMPU

To La Paz and Achacachi

Ancoma

PICO SCHULZE

HUAYNA ILLAMPU

Lakathiya

Sorata

N

10km

0

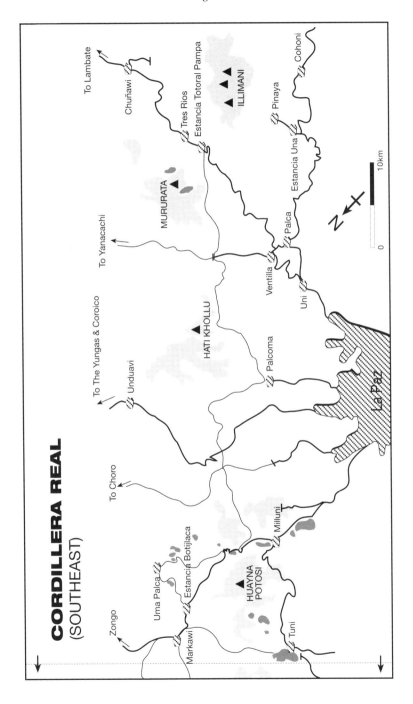

CORDILLERA REAL
(SOUTHEAST)

ACCESS

In general, La Paz is the starting point for any climb in the cordillera. Base camp for most routes can be reached in 1 day from La Paz by crossing the Altiplano using the La Paz–Huarina asphalt road until the appropriate access road or track is reached. The main exception is climbs in the Ancohuma-Illampu massif where the starting point is Sorata, which is 4 hours by bus from La Paz. From Sorata, it is generally at least 2 days on foot to base camp.

MAPS

In addition to the O'Brien map, IGM 1:50,000 sheets are available for Sorata and the Cordillera Real southeast of Jankho Laya. Guzmán Córdova publishes maps to Ancohuma-Illampu, Negruni-Condoriri, Huayna Potosí, and Illimani.

The mountains of the Cordillera Real are listed from north to south, apart from Huayna Illampu, which is described after Pico Schulze because they share the same approach.

ancohuma-illampu massif

The northern end of the Cordillera Real is marked by the Ancohuma-Illampu massif, which is large and complicated, with more than thirty peaks over 5,000 m/16,000 ft. The best maps to use for the massif are the DAV Cordillera Real Nord (Illampu) and the IGM Sorata 5846 I.

Access

Unlike the rest of the peaks in the range, the starting point for any climb in the Ancohuma-Illampu massif is Sorata. This beautiful colonial town, situated at a pleasant 2,678 m/8,786 ft, is noticeably warmer than La Paz.

At various times during its history, Sorata has been a center for the cultivation of coca, quinine, and rubber. From a vantage point among the giant palm trees on the main square, it is possible to see Illampu.

The town has a selection of hotels, and justifiably the most popular is the rambling Residencial Sorata on the plaza, with its great breakfasts for US$2. Slightly out of town is the more modern and expensive German-run Hotel Copacabana. Most of the restaurants are located on the plaza, but they are also dotted around town, including the not-to-be-missed Ristorante Italiano. The food here is as good as the service is slow, but you can use the time to watch the sunset over the valley of the Río San Cristobal from the terrace. Fresh bread is available in Sorata, and a small market sells some fruit and vegetables. La Paz has a far greater selection of packaged food, however, and you should make your purchases there. Some supplies, for example, bread, can sometimes be bought in the villages of Ancoma and Cocoyo, but don't rely on it.

Buses from La Paz to Sorata leave from the corner of Calle Manuel Bustillos and Avenida Kollasuyo, 2 blocks above Cementerio, every day between 6:00 A.M. and 3:00 P.M. Reservations are recommended for travel on Friday. The journey takes 4 hours and costs US$2. Sit on the right for the best views of the Cordillera Real. Remember to take your passport with you for the military checkpoint at Achacachi.

Buses from Sorata to La Paz leave from the main square every day between 5:00 A.M. and 4:00 P.M.

All the routes out of Sorata are difficult to follow because the large number of paths in the area make it a challenge to pick the right one. In addition, all the routes climb out very steeply. To overcome these two problems, hire mules for US$8 per day.

The Sorata guides and porters association has its office opposite the Residencial Sorata on the corner of the main plaza. The association can provide mules and/or porters to any base camp in the area. However, at the time of this writing only two porters had experience using crampons. Before hiring anyone to porter on ice, check that they have experience, boots suitable to take crampons, and glacier glasses.

PICO SCHULZE
(NEVADO DE COTAÑA)

5,943 m/19,498 ft

1928, ERWIN HEIN (AUSTRIA), ALFRED HORESCHOWSKY, HUGO HÖRTNAGEL, AND HANS PFANN (GERMANY) VIA THE NORTHWEST FACE

Pico Schulze stands northwest of Illampu across the high camp above Aguas Calientes. It has been climbed from three sides; the south face has the hardest routes. Anyone who climbs Illampu sees Pico Schulze, but because of its sub-6,000 m/20,000 ft height, it tends to be ignored in favor of its higher neighbor.

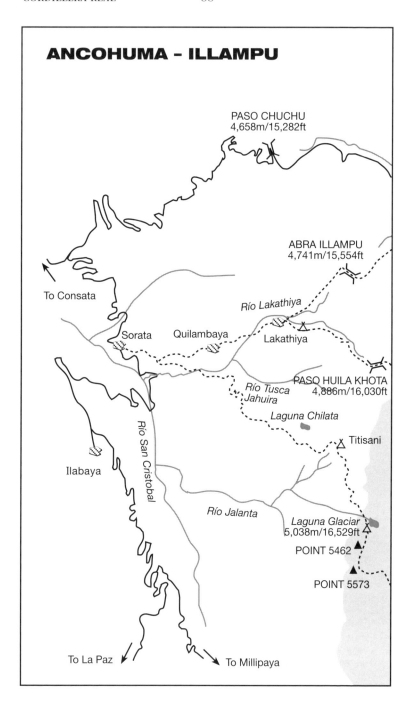

ANCOHUMA - ILLAMPU

PASO CHUCHU
4,658m/15,282ft

ABRA ILLAMPU
4,741m/15,554ft

To Consata

Río Lakathiya

Sorata   Quilambaya   Lakathiya

PASO HUILA KHOTA
4,886m/16,030ft

Río Tusca
Jahuira

Laguna Chilata

Titisani

Río San Cristobal

Ilabaya

Río Jalanta

Laguna Glaciar
5,038m/16,529ft

POINT 5462

POINT 5573

To La Paz   To Millipaya

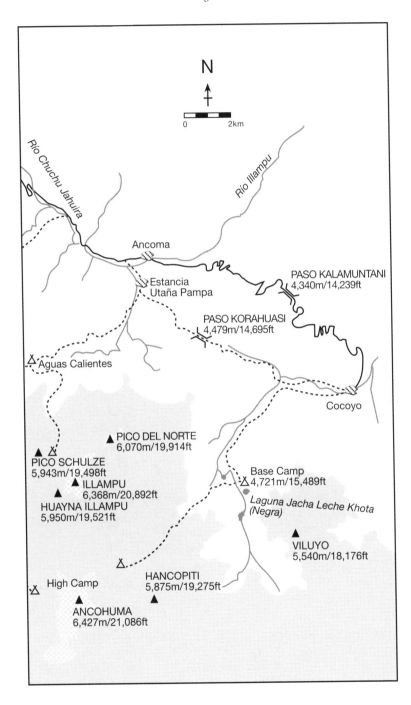

Approach via Aguas Calientes

1) Hire a jeep to travel from Sorata to Ancoma, which takes 3 hours and costs US$55. Irregular jeep trips run between Sorata and Ancoma, and you might be able to share one of these if you are a small group. Ask at the guides and porters association for up-to-date information.

For travel from Ancoma, it is recommended to hire mules (US$8 per mule) for the 3-hour walk up to Aguas Calientes via Estancia Utaña Pampa. From Ancoma, head back up the road to Estancia Utaña Pampa, and then follow paths up the left-hand side of the valley. Cross to the right-hand side of the valley before reaching the plain below the terminal moraines. Aguas Calientes (4,600 m/15,092 ft) is a misnomer—they are tepid and greasy, and the frogs croak all night—but the water runs clear. This is the highest point you can get to with mules.

2) For a cheaper approach that requires more physical effort, go directly to Aguas Calientes from Sorata by foot, which takes 2 days.

Day 1: From Sorata, walk up to Lakathiya at 4,000 m/13,120 ft, which takes 4 hours with mules at US$8 each. Camp 15 minutes above the village in a plain on the way to Paso Huila Khota (4,886 m/16,030 ft).

Day 2: Porters are available for hire for US$5 each for the 3-hour walk from Lakathiya to the pass and the 45-minute descent to Aguas Calientes (4,600 m/15,092 ft) on the other side.

An acclimatized group could walk from Sorata to Aguas Calientes in 1 day (with mules to Lakathiya and then porters to Aguas Calientes), but remember the ascent is 2,208 m/7,244 ft from Sorata to Paso Huila Khota. Similarly, the descent from Aguas Calientes to Sorata with porters and then mules is also possible in 1 day. It takes only 5 hours, but you will feel the effect on your knees.

From Aguas Calientes facing up valley, go up the slope on the left. Drop and then contour around into the next valley, and head up the right-hand side through the cairn epidemic. Drop down to the moraine on the right-hand side of the glacier, and follow the moraine ridge until it meets the glacier. Join the very broken glacier, and work a way up the right-hand side until you reach the flat—although crevassed—area for a high camp immediately below the Northwest Face of Illampu (5,600 m/18,400 ft) in 5 to 7 hours from Aguas Calientes. (The descent is an easy 3 hours and well worth the effort to avoid a second night at high camp on the glacier.)

SOUTHEAST FACE ROUTE

Grade II/AD, 55°, 343 m/1,125 ft

1987 (?)

From the flat part of the glacier below the Illampu Northwest Headwall, find the best place to cross the bergschrund, and move up the face heading for the broad gully leading to the summit.

Descent: Same or follow the Traverse (see below)

SOUTH–NORTH TRAVERSE

Grade III/AD+, 55°, 343 m/1,125 ft

SEPTEMBER 3, 1997, JEAN-MARC DUNSTHEIMER (BELGIUM) AND JOHN WALMSLEY (U.K.)

From base camp, climb up onto the south ridge, meeting it at the point marked 5,765 m on the DAV map. Pass the rock section, and follow the knife-edge ridge to the summit, watching out for the cornice. From the summit, descend northward to reach a flatter area, and then rappel one or two rope lengths toward the right down one of the rocky couloirs to reach the lower snow slopes. Follow a ramp back down to the base camp glacier.

■ ■ ■

Approach via Titisani

From Sorata at 2,678 m/8,786 ft, it is a steady hike up to the abandoned mine buildings of Titisani (4,400 m/14,400 ft), which is due west of Pico Schulze. This takes 6 hours with mules, but you must carry your packs for the last 25 minutes. The mules cannot do the short steep descent to the abandoned mine buildings.

NORTHWEST FACE ROUTE

1928, ERWIN HEIN (AUSTRIA), ALFRED HORESCHOWSKY, HUGO HÖRTNAGEL, AND HANS PFANN (GERMANY)

From the abandoned mine, head up over rocks and then scree before rejoining the rock that leads to the glacier, well to the left (north) of the summit. Move up the glacier heading for the broad ridge that leads to the summit.

Descent: Same

PICO SCHULZE
SOUTH-NORTH TRAVERSE

SOUTHEAST FACE ROUTE

FROM BASE CAMP BELOW ILLAMPU NORMAL ROUTE

PICO SCHULZE
WEST FACE
FROM TITISANI

NORTHWEST FACE ROUTE

■ ■ ■

Approach via Laguna Glaciar

Travel from Titisani to excellent camping on the western shore of Laguna Glaciar (5,038 m/16,529 ft) takes 3 hours with porters. Follow an often indistinct path that rises gently until it reaches rocky slabs. The route gets steeper immediately before you arrive at Laguna Glaciar.

From Laguna Glaciar, head up the glacier working a way around and through the many crevasses. Stay on the left-hand side of the glacier to reach a bivouac site on the flat glacier below the Southwest Face at about 5,500 m/18,000 ft.

SOUTH PYRAMID SOUTHWEST FACE ROUTE

Grade III/D-, 70°, 600 m/1,950 ft, 10 hours

MAY 1973, ALAIN MESILI (FRANCE) AND ERNESTO SÁNCHEZ (BOLIVIA)

This hard and beautiful route is not as objectively safe as it was in the early 1970s. Head straight up the face. The angle eases to bring you to the Pico Schulze summit ridge.

Descent: Rappel back down, or descend the Northwest Face of Pico Schulze, which takes you down the other side of the mountain to the Aguas Calientes campsite.

HUAYNA ILLAMPU

5,950 m/19,521 ft

1964, N. CASTILLO, T. INAGAWA, AND K. SUSUKI VIA THE WEST FACE

Known as "Little Illampu" in Aymara, this peak lies to the west of Illampu itself. Routes on the west and especially the south faces are steep and hard.

Approach

See Approach via Laguna Glaciar above.

SOUTHWEST FACE ROUTE

Grade IV (5.9)/TD (VI), 70°, 700 m/2,300 ft, 9 hours

MAY 1973, ALAIN MESILI (FRANCE) AND ERNESTO SÁNCHEZ (BOLIVIA)

From the bivouac site, skirt around to reach the broad snow ramp that leads up to the bottom of the route. The start is steep, but the angle

PICO SCHULZE, HUAYNA ILLAMPU, & ILLAMPU
FROM ABOVE LAGUNA GLACIAR

SOUTHWEST FACE ROUTE

SOUTH PYRAMID
SOUTHWEST FACE ROUTE

eases halfway up. There is an easy snowfield to cross before you reach the summit.

Descent: Rappel or downclimb the Northwest Headwall to the Aguas Calientes camp.

ILLAMPU

6,368 m/20,892 ft

JUNE 7, 1928, ERWIN HEIN (AUSTRIA), ALFRED HORESCHOWSKY,

HUGO HÖRTNAGEL, AND HANS PFANN (GERMANY)

Big, high, and complicated, Illampu boasts the hardest normal route of any of the 6,000 m/20,000 ft peaks in Bolivia. This makes any climb on the mountain serious—there is no easy way off—and the hardest routes yet climbed in Bolivia have been done on the mountain.

Approach and Access

See Pico Schulze above.

SOUTHWEST RIDGE ROUTE

Grade III-/AD, 65°, 800 m/2,600 ft, 6–9 hours

JUNE 7, 1928, ERWIN HEIN (AUSTRIA), ALFRED HORESCHOWSKY,

HUGO HÖRTNAGEL, AND HANS PFANN (GERMANY)

From high camp, head straight up the 300 m/1,000 ft Northwest Headwall (60°) to reach the saddle between Illampu and Huayna Illampu in 2–3 hours. The headwall is icy later in the season and can have a huge bergschrund. It is steeper to the left of the rock band.

From the saddle, go left and follow the broad and often exposed Southwest Ridge at 30–40°. The 80 m/260 ft section on the final part of the summit ridge is very exposed and steep (65°). Follow the ridge to attain the summit in 3–5 hours from the saddle.

Descent: Same. Snow conditions deteriorate in the afternoon as the sun shines on the headwall, so it is important to start back early.

■ ■ ■

Approach via Laguna Glaciar

For the approach, see Pico Schulze above.

These routes are steep and serious. The exact line depends on the state of the seracs that threaten large parts of Illampu's southwest face.

Illampu rising out of the clouds, as seen from Ancohuma, Cordillera Real

GERMAN ROUTE

Grade III+/D, 60°, 1,000 m/3,300 ft, 7 hours

JULY 27, 1967, HORST CAHA AND WERNER KABL (GERMANY)

Climb up Illampu's southwest face to join the Southwest Ridge above the Northwest Headwall, and then follow the ridge to the summit. Paul Drummond, writing in the *Alpine Journal* (1985), described the route as "exposed climbing over hard ice covered in several inches of powdery, unsupporting snow. Our route finding was blind; up one curve, round the next ice bulge and so on."

Descent: Either downclimb, or rappel the same route, or drop down the Northwest Headwall. Although this is easier and quicker, it leaves you on the other side of the mountain.

SOUTH FACE ROUTE

1983

This route is the most direct line possible to reach the southeast ridge shortly before it joins the southwest summit ridge. Follow the ridge to the summit.

Descent: Same as German Route

ILLAMPU
SOUTHWEST RIDGE ROUTE
FROM HIGH CAMP

NORTHWEST HEADWALL

ILLAMPU
SOUTH FACE FROM ANCOHUMA

GERMAN ROUTE

SOUTH FACE ROUTE

ANCOHUMA
(JANKOHUMA, JANQ'UMA, HANCOUMA)

6,427 m/21,086 ft

JUNE 11, 1919, RUDOLF DIENST AND ADOLF SCHULZE (GERMANY)

Maps: DAV Cordillera Real Nord (Illampu); IGM Sorata 5846 I
and Warizata 5846 II

Generations of Bolivian and other cartographers have claimed that Ancohuma is the highest mountain in Bolivia and given it heights of up to 7,014 m/23,012 ft, which would make it the only mountain in the world over 7,000 m/23,000 ft outside the Himalayas. It is generally held that Aconcagua in Argentina is the highest mountain outside the Himalayas at 6,960 m/22,834 ft. However, it is true that Ancohuma is the highest peak of the Ancohuma-Illampu massif.

Approach via Laguna Glaciar

See Pico Schulze (above) for directions on how to get to Titisani and then on to Laguna Glaciar.

Normally, porters arrive at Laguna Glaciar the next day for the 3-hour climb to the edge of the glacier at Point 5573. However, if you are acclimatized, it makes sense to continue up to the top of the hill above Laguna Glaciar at 5,200 m/17,000 ft on the same day that you reach the

Camp III (approx. 5,600m) on the west side of Ancohuma, Cordillera Real

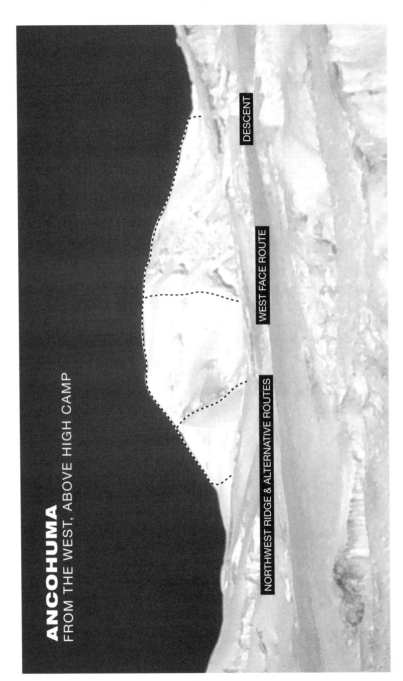

ANCOHUMA
FROM THE WEST, ABOVE HIGH CAMP

DESCENT

WEST FACE ROUTE

NORTHWEST RIDGE & ALTERNATIVE ROUTES

lake. Unless porters have boots, crampons, and glacier glasses, they should not be allowed to carry packs on the glacier.

From the western end of the lake, head right and follow the scree at the edge of the glacier. Below Point 5462 on the DAV map, cross a short section of glacier and follow the right-hand side of the glacier next to the rocks toward Point 5573. From here, rope up and pick a way across the heavily crevassed glacier, aiming to get as far across as possible and set up camp on the glacier at about 5,800 m/19,000 ft. There are some clear glacial streams and ponds below the big broken step up to the final approach glacier. From the high camp glacier, plod up to the base of the summit and pick a route.

NORTHWEST RIDGE ROUTE

Grade III/AD+, 60°, 650 m/2,100 ft, 6 hours

Climb up the glacier, heading for the left-hand side of the summit lump. Either go straight for the ridge or work a way up the face to join it. The ridge is spectacularly exposed, dropping hundreds of meters below the point where you join it from the west. From this vantage point, you have fantastic views of Illampu. At the top of the ridge, join the summit plateau, and keep plodding until you reach the highest point.

Descent: Either rappel straight down the face from the summit or head down to the col southwest of the summit and descend the Southwest Face to reach the glacier below. Then head down to rejoin your tracks back to high camp.

WEST FACE ROUTE

Grade II/AD, 60°, 650 m/2,100 ft, 6 hours

This route is a straightforward one. From below the summit lump, head straight up the middle, avoiding some very large and obvious crevasses which are often filled in.

Descent: Same as for the Northwest Ridge Route

■ ■ ■

Approach via Laguna Jacha Leche Khota (Negra)

This approach is the traditional and the longest way in used to climb Ancohuma.

Reaching the summit plateau, Northwest Ridge, Ancohuma, Cordillera Real

Day 1: Travel from Sorata to Cocoyo takes 5 hours by jeep for US$80. Once in Cocoyo, make arrangements for llamas—which carry loads of only 12 kgs/26 lbs each—for the next day.

Day 2: Walk from Cocoyo to base camp at Laguna Jacha Leche Khota (Negra) (4,721 m/15,489 ft) takes 6 hours.

Alternatively, if you are walking and/or using mules from Sorata:

Day 1: Travel from Sorata (2,678 m/8,786 ft) to Lakathiya (4,000 m/13,120 ft) takes 4 hours.

Day 2: Travel from Lakathiya to Abra Illampu (4,741 m/15,554 ft) takes 2 hours. The descent toward Ancoma (3,784 m/12,415 ft) takes another 3 hours.

Day 3: Travel from Ancoma to Cocoyo (3,512 m/11,522 ft) via Paso Korahuasi (4,479 m/14,695 ft) takes 5 hours.

SOUTHWEST FACE NORMAL ROUTE

Grade I/PD, 45°, 1,000 m/3,300 ft, 7–9 hours

JUNE 11, 1919, RUDOLF DIENST AND ADOLF SCHULZE (GERMANY)

This route is long but not very difficult. Head up the right-hand side of the face to reach the summit plateau, and keep plodding until you reach the highest point.

Descent: Same

central section of cordillera real

The central section stretches from the Calzada Pass, south of the Ancohuma-Illampu massif, to the Zongo Pass, south of Huayna Potosí. It includes the mountains Chearoco, Chachacomani, and Jankho Laya, the Condoriri Group, and Huayna Potosí. The section north of Condoriri is the least-visited part of the Cordillera Real. In contrast, Condoriri and Huayna Potosí are the most visited areas of the range.

CHEAROCO
(CH'IYRUQ'U, CORPAPATU)

6,127 m/20,101 ft

JULY 25, 1928, ALFRED HORESCHOWSKY AND HUGO HÖRTNAGEL (AUSTRIA)

FROM THE WEST

Map: Only O'Brien covers this area

Chearoco is a complicated mountain with long routes. By far the main problem with any way up or down the peak is picking a route through the innumerable crevasses, a time-consuming exercise, especially at the end of a long day. A lot of people appear to have tried finding a crevasse-free route because the mountain has been climbed by seemingly all possible routes.

Route descriptions are given from the east and from the west; crossing the large glaciated col area between Chearoco and Kelluani gives access to the other side. Some routes, such as the Southeast Ridge, can be done from either side.

Warning: Gringos and nonlocal Bolivians have had innumerable problems (ranging from assault to routine hassling and road blocks) with the peasants to the west of this area who have had a bad reputation since pre-Inca times and seem determined to maintain it.

Access from the West

Take a bus from the Cementerio district of La Paz to Achacachi or Peñas (US$2, 2 hours), and then make arrangements for a pick up for the 2-hour drive or for animals for the 2-day walk-in to base camp going in via the valley of the Río Kelluani.

Alternatively, find a driver willing to drive in to the area above the small collection of farms that make up Kelluani, which takes 3½ hours from La Paz and costs US$200.

CHEAROCO
FROM THE SOUTHWEST

SOUTHEAST RIDGE ROUTE

SOUTHWEST SPUR ROUTE

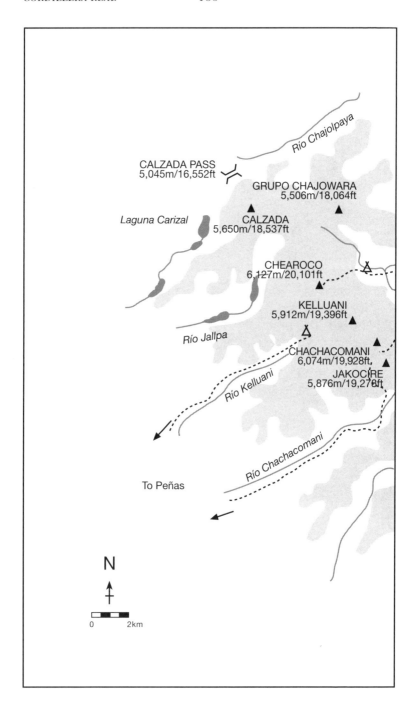

Río Chajolpaya

CALZADA PASS
5,045m/16,552ft

GRUPO CHAJOWARA
5,506m/18,064ft

Laguna Carizal

CALZADA
5,650m/18,537ft

CHEAROCO
6,127m/20,101ft

KELLUANI
5,912m/19,396ft

Río Jallpa

CHACHACOMANI
6,074m/19,928ft

JAKOCIRE
5,876m/19,278ft

Río Kelluani

Río Chachacomani

To Peñas

N

0   2km

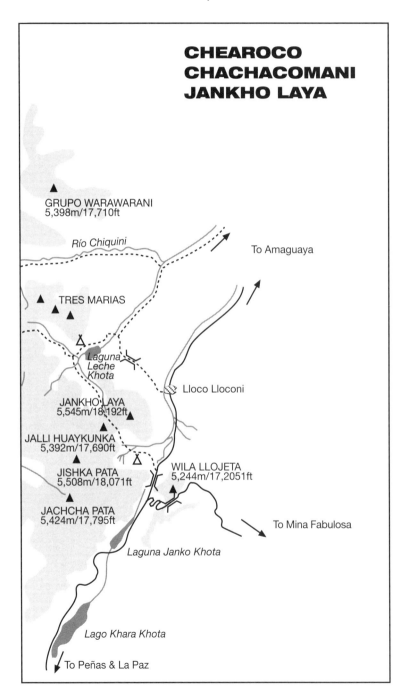

CHEAROCO
CHACHACOMANI
JANKHO LAYA

GRUPO WARAWARANI
5,398m/17,710ft

Río Chiquini

To Amaguaya

TRES MARIAS

Laguna Leche Khota

Lloco Lloconi

JANKHO LAYA
5,545m/18,192ft

JALLI HUAYKUNKA
5,392m/17,690ft

JISHKA PATA
5,508m/18,071ft

WILA LLOJETA
5,244m/17,2051ft

JACHCHA PATA
5,424m/17,795ft

To Mina Fabulosa

Laguna Janko Khota

Lago Khara Khota

To Peñas & La Paz

Approach

From the end of the track, walk up to the ridge above Kelluani, and then drop down along the left-hand side of the valley to reach the boggy valley bottom. It takes 3½ hours to follow it to its end, where there is a sedimented lake, some clear streams, and a flat area for camping (4,750 m/15,600 ft). Climb up the moraine ridge on the right-hand side of the glacier, and then join the glacier after 1 hour. Sometimes a clear glacial stream runs down the middle of the glacier.

SOUTHWEST SPUR ROUTE

Grade III/AD+, 60°, 1,300 m/4,250 ft

JUNE 26, 1978, GIUSEPPE FERRARI, ANGELO GELMI, FRANCO GUGIATTI, GIUSEPPE
LANFRANCONI, KIKI MARMORI, MARCO VITALE, AND COSIMO ZAPPELLI (ITALY)

An ice slope on this route leads to mixed climbing and then on to the summit ice mushroom. Look for a break, and go through it to reach the summit.

Descent: Same

WEST FACE ROUTE

Grade III/AD+, 55°, 900 m/3,000 ft

JUNE 1982, DANIEL BURRIEZA AND RODOLFO CRISPO (ARGENTINA)

From a bivouac at the bottom of the face at 5,200 m/17,000 ft, head up to the south summit (up to 50°), and then traverse to the north summit.

Descent: The route is via the Southwest Spur, which has convex slopes that make it difficult to see the way down.

■ ■ ■

Access from the East

Hire a jeep for the trip from La Paz to Lloco Lloconi (see Chacha-comani approach, Option 2), which takes 4 hours and costs US$200. If you want llamas to carry your packs, be prepared to camp at Lloco Lloconi or lower down the valley, and set off the next day to Laguna Leche Khota.

Approach

Head up and over the pass above Lloco Lloconi, and descend on the other side. From here, turn left, and move up to Laguna Leche Khota and camp, about 5 hours from Lloco Lloconi. The lake is sedimented, but there is a clear stream at the top right-hand side of the lake. On the next day, head up the valley between Chachacomani and the Tres Marias Group, cross the glaciated pass, and descend to base camp in the valley of the Río Chiquini between the Tres Marias and Chajowara Groups.

SOUTHEAST RIDGE ROUTE

Grade III/AD+, 50°, 900 m/1,000 ft

AUGUST 19, 1962, JOHN FLOODPAGE, RONALD HUNTER, AND EDWARD QUICKE (U.K.)

Work a way up to the ridge, and then follow it to the summit. The route is not as smooth going as it looks—there are a lot of crevasses.

Descent: Same

CHACHACOMANI

6,074 m/19,928 ft

AUGUST 1, 1947, FRIEDRICH FRITZ AND GUENTHER BUCCHOLTZ (GERMANY), GUSTAVO
MOELLER, DOUGLAS MOORE, ISAIAS PAZ, AND GUILLERMO SANJINÉS (BOLIVIA)

Map: Only O'Brien covers this area

Beautiful from afar and difficult to get near to, Chachacomani's distinctive South Face is very clear from the Altiplano, and it led to the nineteenth-century traveler and explorer Sir Martin Conway's reference to the mountain as "Chisel Peak." The best lines are on the South Face, but the "Macho Mountain" (the literal Aymara translation) has been climbed from most directions. To the northwest of the mountain is a large flat glacier that links the mountain to Kelluani.

Warning: Gringos and nonlocal Bolivians have had innumerable problems (ranging from assault to routine hassling and road blocks) with the peasants to the west of this area who have had a bad reputation since pre-Inca times and seem determined to maintain it.

Access

No public transportation is available to the Chachacomani area.

Option 1: Hire a jeep from La Paz and travel via Peñas to the Hichukhota valley. Continue up the road to the top of the Hichukhota valley, passing impressively high above Laguna Khara Khota. At the top of the valley, where the old road continues up to the right to Mina Fabulosa, follow the new road up to the left, go over the pass

Dawn, Chachacomani, Cordillera Real

(4,980 m/16,360 ft), and get dropped off at the bottom of the zigzags, about 15 minutes by jeep below the Paso Mullu Apacheta area. Total journey time is 3½ hours and costs US$200.

Approach

Walk from the road, and contour to the left around the boggy area to reach the bottom of the boulder moraine in ½ hour. Head up the left-hand side of the moraine to reach a boulder moraine ridge in another ½ hour. Follow the ridge to a lake (4,940 m/16,200 ft), and then either head up the rock and scree on the left-hand side of the glacier or walk up the glacier itself to reach the col (5,140 m/16,860 ft) in under 2 hours. Drop down into the valley on the other side. The first camping area with clear running water is 45 minutes below the col. About 2 hours below the col, you arrive above Laguna Leche Khota.

Option 2: A longer but easier option not involving a glacier crossing: instead of getting out of the jeep opposite Jankho Laya, continue down the new road for 10 minutes to reach the cluster of farm buildings called Lloco Lloconi. Cross the river, follow the path up and over the pass, drop down and then turn left and head up to Laguna Leche Khota. It is possible to hire llamas in Lloco Lloconi, but not many people do so. The local people do not have much experience working with tourists. If you want to hire llamas, be prepared to camp at Lloco Lloconi and then set off the next day.

For either option, from Laguna Leche Khota head up the boulder moraine between Chachacomani and the Tres Marias Group to arrive at possible campsites in 1 hour. From here head left to the col, which is reached in 2 hours and has views of Lake Titicaca. From the col, move up to arrive below the South Face, staying to the left-hand side of the broken glacier to avoid the worst of the crevasses.

SOUTH FACE NORMAL ROUTES
Grade II/AD, 55°, 800 m/2,600 ft

A big bergschrund crosses most of the face, especially later in the season. Pick a line close to the center of the face while avoiding the seracs above to reach the summit ridge. Follow the ridge toward the right to the summit.

Descent: Same

SOUTHEAST RIDGE ROUTE
Grade II/AD, 50°, 800 m/2,600 ft

This route is more direct and steeper than the South Face Route. It goes straight to the summit, starting at the right-hand side of the face.

Descent: South Face Normal Routes

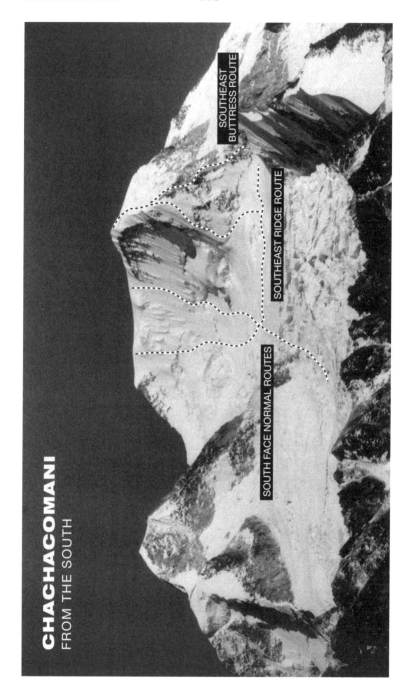

CHACHACOMANI
FROM THE SOUTH

SOUTHEAST BUTTRESS ROUTE

SOUTHEAST RIDGE ROUTE

SOUTH FACE NORMAL ROUTES

SOUTHEAST BUTTRESS ROUTE
Grade III+ (5.7)/D (V), 70°, 800 m/2,600 ft
AUGUST 1, 1989, GEOF BARTRAM, JOHN CULBERSON, LARRY HALL,
AND MATT KOEHLER (U.S.)

This is the hardest route so far recorded on Chachacomani. Mixed climbing brings you to the Southeast Ridge line before continuing to the summit.

Descent: South Face Normal Routes

JANKHO LAYA
(JANQ'U LAYA, JANKHO LACAYA, JANCORACAYA)
5,545 m/18,192 ft
SEPTEMBER 23, 1970, TAKAYA TAKESHITA AND NORIO YAMAMOTO (JAPAN)

Maps: IGM Lago Khara Kkota 5945 IV (This map does not show the new road that continues north and crosses the pass to the west of Cerro Wila Llojeta.)

Walter Guzmán Córdova Negruni-Condoriri

Jankho Laya now enjoys easy access, but the mountain is suffering from severe glacial retreat because of its location on the eastern side of the cordillera and its close proximity to the jungle. The summit is now a 2 m/6 ft high lump of rock (unless it has snowed a lot) with a very long drop off on the other side and a very sharp 1 m/3 ft crest, which makes sitting down for those summit photos uncomfortable. Neither the French 1978 expedition, which thoroughly ticked the mountain, nor Mesili in his 1984 guidebook mention the rock, which suggests it is a child of the 1990s.

Access

No public transportation is available to the Jankho Laya area. Hire a jeep from La Paz and travel via Peñas to the Hichukhota valley. Continue up the road to the top of the Hichukhota valley, passing impressively high above Laguna Khara Khota. At the top of the valley, where the old road continues up to the right to Mina Fabulosa, follow the new road up to the left, go over the pass (4,980 m/16,340 ft), and get dropped off at the bottom of the zigzags, about 15 minutes by jeep below the Paso Mullu Apacheta area. Total journey time is 3½ hours and costs US$200.

Approach

From the road, it takes ½ hour to walk to base camp, which is situated at the far end of the flat stream-crossed grassy area at 4,600 m/15,100 ft

below an old granite boulder field. Keep to the left-hand side of the grassy area to reduce the necessity for bog-trotting. Although the main stream is full of sediment, a couple of clear streams are found in the base camp area.

For routes other than the Normal Route, it is worth walking up the left-hand side of the boulder field above and then continuing on to reach a flat grassy area called the Vinowara Plain (4,800 m/15,750 ft), which is opposite the west face. This trip takes another 1½ hours from the normal base camp. The names of the members of the French 1978 expedition are carved in a rock at the entrance to the plain.

SOUTH FACE/EAST RIDGE (NORMAL) ROUTE
Grade II (5.4)/AD (III), 60°, 700 m/2,300 ft, 6 hours

Because of the glacial retreat, it is necessary to scramble up granite slabs to reach the bottom of the glacier. There is one short pitch of 50–60° to get on to the glacier, depending on the point you choose to access the glacier. Once on the glacier, work a way up to the East Ridge, avoiding the large and normally obvious crevasses. Follow the ridge to the summit.

Descent: Same

SOUTHEAST RIDGE ROUTE
Grade II/AD, 45°, 800 m/2,600 ft, 6 hours

SEPTEMBER 23, 1970, TAKAYA TAKESHITA AND NORIO YAMAMOTO (JAPAN)

This route is a plod. Start the ridge in the valley near the road, and stick with it, staying on the north side of the ridge. The ridge eventually becomes glacier-covered. Follow it to the summit.

Descent: Same or the Normal Route

SOUTH FACE CENTRAL SPUR ROUTE
Grade IV (5.5)/TD (IV+), 70°, 800 m/2,600 ft, 8 hours

MAY 22, 1978, DANIEL BARRERAS, JEAN-PAUL CHASSAGNE, PIERRE FAUSSURIER, AND PATRICK MURE (FRANCE)

This route follows an impressive line of what now appears to be loose granite, loose snow, and loose ice. The route is clear from the Vinowara

Descending Jankho Laya, Cordillera Real

Plain, which is a better base camp for this particular route. Follow the spur to the summit.

Descent: Normal Route

WEST COL/NORTH FACE ROUTE

Grade II/AD, 45°, 700 m/2,300 ft, 7 hours

MAY 20, 1978, FRANCINE AND JEAN-PAUL CHASSAGNE AND PATRICK MURE (FRANCE)

From the Vinowara Plain, head up the left-hand side of the glacier to the col. From the col, move up and around to reach the North Face. Climb the face to the summit.

Descent: Same or Normal Route

...

CONDORIRI GROUP

This beautiful group has thirteen peaks all over 5,000 m/16,400 ft. Each peak is accessible within 1 day's journey from base camp, which is idyllically situated on the shores of Laguna Chiar Khota ("Black Lake") with views of the striking Cabeza de Condor and its two wings. Hans Ertl described his camp at Condoriri in 1953 as "truly fairylike." Easy access from La Paz, pure snow face and ridge routes plus mixed routes, ranging from easy to extreme, make Condoriri a delightful climbing playground.

Maps

Walter Guzmán Córdova Condoriri-Negruni—but most of the Condoriri Group mountain names are wrong. Four IGM sheets are needed to cover the same area as the Guzmán map: Milluni 5945 II, Peñas 5945 III, Zongo 5945 I, and Lago Khara Khota 5945 IV.

Access and Approach

No public transportation is available to the Condoriri Group area. Hire a jeep for the trip from La Paz to Tuni via Patamanta, which takes 2 hours and costs US$78. Mules (US$6 each) and llamas (US$3 each) are available from Tuni village and from a place shortly before you get

The Condoriri group—Ala Izquierda, Cabeza de Condor, and Ala Derecha —Cordillera Real

CABEZA DE CONDOR

ALA DERECHA

HUALLOMEN

CONDORIRI GROUP A
FROM THE SOUTHEAST

BASE CAMP

LAGUNA CHIAR KHOTA

AGUJA NEGRA
ILUSION
ILUSIONCITA
PIRAMIDE BLANCA
DIENTE
PEQUEÑO ALPAMAYO
TARIJA

CONDORIRI GROUP B
FROM THE SOUTHWEST

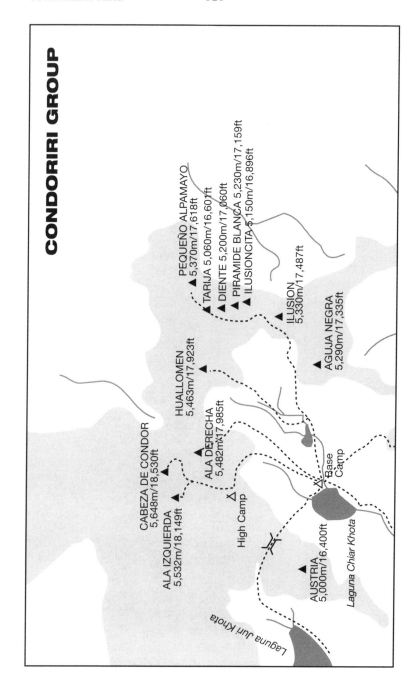

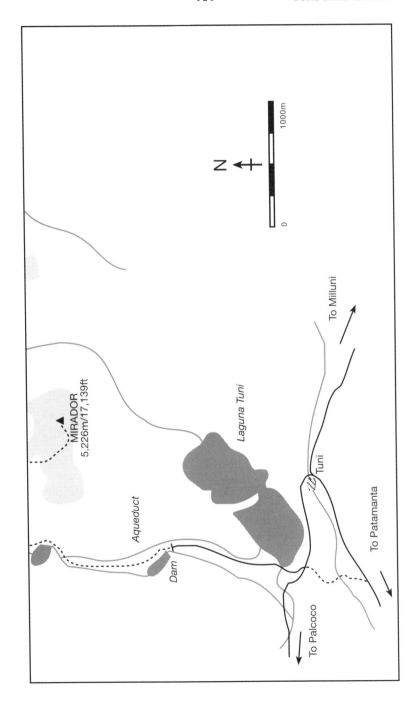

to the village known as Plaza de Mulas for the 3-hour walk-in to base camp at 4,600 m/15,100 ft on the far side of Laguna Chiar Khota. Toilets, a tap with clean water, and camp guards are provided by people from the local community. There is a charge of US$2 per tent per night.

The Condoriri Group peaks are described from left to right as you see them from base camp. The technically uninteresting peaks of Austria, Tarija, Diente, and Mirador are not included—nor is the impressive pile of loose choss called Aguja Negra.

ALA IZQUIERDA
(ALA NORTE, CONDORIRI WEST PEAK)
5,532 m/18,149 ft

JUNE 19, 1963, NICHOLAS COETZEE AND MALCOLM GRIFFIN (SOUTH AFRICA)

Ala Izquierda's distinctive snow wall faces almost due south, so it is always in shadow and the snow does not consolidate, remaining as powder late into the season. Routes on the face get steadily steeper the higher you go, and the rock at either end of the South Face is of very poor quality whether you go up or down it.

It is possible to set up a high camp to shorten the approach to Ala Izquierda routes. See Cabeza de Condor Approach section below.

WEST RIDGE ROUTE
Grade III-/AD+, 60°, 600 m/1,950 ft

JUNE 14, 1970, JOHN HUDSON, ROMAN LABA (U.S.),
AND ELSPETH AND ROGER WHEWELL (U.K.)

Make a way around the western end of Ala Izquierda until you find a climbable way up to the West Ridge. Follow the ridge to the west summit, and continue along it to the higher summit.

Descent: Same or see South Face Route

SOUTH FACE ROUTE
Grade III/D-, 60°, 600 m/1,950 ft, 3 hours from high camp

SEPTEMBER 14, 1979, ALAIN MESILI, FREDERIC PIMIENTA, AND ANSELME BAUD (FRANCE)

This route is straightforward. Either climb up to the left (slightly shorter) or to the right of the central seracs to reach the ridge. Turn

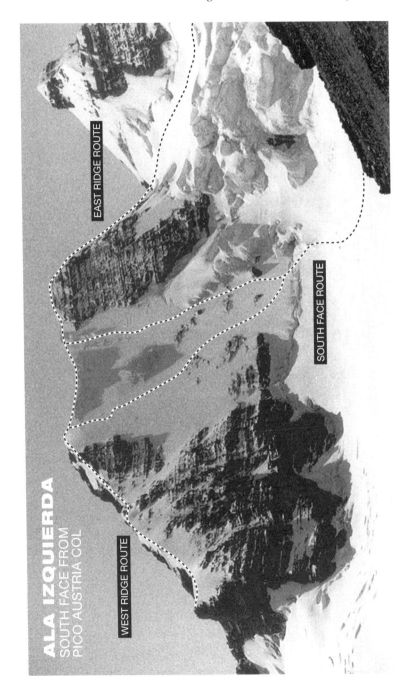

ALA IZQUIERDA
SOUTH FACE FROM
PICO AUSTRIA COL

EAST RIDGE ROUTE

SOUTH FACE ROUTE

WEST RIDGE ROUTE

right, and follow the ridge to reach the highest point.

Descent: The descent from this route is a nightmare. If downclimbing does not appeal to you, there are two options: Scramble and rappel two or three rope lengths down the extremely loose rock of the east ridge and face to the col between Ala Izquierda and Cabeza de Condor. From here, pick a way through the crevasses to join the Normal Route to and from Cabeza de Condor. Alternatively, go back along the Ala Izquierda summit ridge to the left-hand end, and downclimb or rappel 500 m/ 1,650 ft to reach the foot of the face.

EAST RIDGE ROUTE

Grade II/AD, 55°, 300 m/1,000 ft

JUNE 19, 1963, NICHOLAS COETZEE AND MALCOLM GRIFFIN (SOUTH AFRICA)

From the col between Ala Izquierda and Cabeza de Condor, follow the mixed loose snow and rock ridge to the summit. (See Cabeza de Condor below for the route to the col.)

Descent: Same or see South Face Route

CABEZA DE CONDOR
(CONDORIRI, GRAN CONDORIRI)

5,648 m/18,530 ft

APRIL 1940, WILFRID KÜHM (GERMANY), SOLO

Cabeza de Condor, or the "Bolivian Matterhorn" as Hans Ertl called it, is one of the most striking mountains in the Cordillera Real. Seen from base camp, the Southeast Face appears to be almost overhanging, while from the pass to the north of Pico Austria the Cabeza is a great rock and ice spike. This peak is generally climbed via the Normal Route or the Directisima, but it has also been climbed from the other sides, which have steep routes.

Approach

A high camp is located 3 hours from base camp if you want to shorten the climbs of Cabeza de Condor and Ala Izquierda. From base camp, head northwest along paths toward the Cabeza, move up a small scree slope, and then follow a scree ridge toward the left to reach the bottom of the "scree slope from hell" in 1 hour. The slope is followed to the bitter end, which is sometimes made up of tricky ice, loose rock, and mud.

Ala Izquierda and Cabeza de Condor from above Laguna Juri Khota, Cordillera Real

The ascent takes an hour or so depending on your scree-ascending abilities. Up to the left are a series of rock ledges, which provide comfortable west-facing—late sunshine—platforms for camping.

The degree of unpleasantness involved in using the scree slope from hell has provoked more ways of avoiding it, including the following options: (1) from the base of the scree slope, head horizontally across right to join one of the snow gullies heading up to the glacier; (2) walk up the path to the pass to the northeast of Pico Austria, and then drop down to the glacier and head up on the right-hand side of the glacier; and (3) access via the valley of the Río Laurauani and Laguna Juri Khota.

SOUTHWEST RIDGE NORMAL ROUTE

Grade III/AD+, 55°, 400 m/1,300 ft, 4 hours from high camp

APRIL 1940, WILFRID KÜHM (GERMANY), SOLO

This route follows a classic alpine ridge line and is one of the best routes in Bolivia. From the top of the scree slope from hell, move up the glacier toward the Cabeza. Either follow the Southwest Ridge from the start or go along the base of the Cabeza until you reach a hidden snow gully 1½ hours from high camp. The gully is broad at the bottom but increasingly narrow toward the top where it joins the ridge, and it can be full of water ice and loose rock. From the top of the gully, turn

CABEZA DE CONDOR (CONDORIRI)
FROM BASE CAMP

DIRECTISIMA SOUTHEAST FACE ROUTE

SOUTHWEST RIDGE
NORMAL ROUTE

right and follow the ridge to the summit. The ridge is exposed on both sides and is made up of a series of steep sections linked by narrow and airy snow ridges, with one rock step that is trickier on the way down.

Descent: Same

DIRECTISIMA SOUTHEAST FACE ROUTE

Grade IV/D+, 65°, 350 m/1,150 ft, 2 hours

SEPTEMBER 18, 1973, JOSÉ FERRARI, ANGELO GELMI (ITALY), AND ALAIN MESILI (FRANCE)

From the base of the Cabeza, pick the most direct snowy line that goes up the center of the face, topping out to the left (south) of the summit. Later in the season there are often rock bands across the face (5.7/V), and the bergschrund opens up. If the bergschrund is too big to cross, it is usually possible to traverse into the route from the hidden couloir.

Descent: Normal Route

ALA DERECHA
(ALA SUR, CONDORIRI SUR)

5,482 m/17,985 ft

JULY 1964 (YUGOSLAVIA)

Ala Derecha presents four imposing gullies which provide Scottish-style mixed climbing at high altitudes. From right to left the gullies are known as the following: Gully 1/Mesili Route, Gully 2, Gully 3, and Gully 4/Colibri Route. Colibri is the hardest and most-often climbed route. Gully 1/Mesili Route, obvious from the walk-in, now has a vertical rock start to a sloping snow ledge.

Approach

From base camp, head northeast up valley, and then make your way toward the left to the glacier below Ala Derecha. Follow this glacier to the bottom of the routes.

GULLY 1/MESILI ROUTE

Grade IV+/TD, 70°, 500 m/1,650 ft

SEPTEMBER 21, 1976, ALAIN MESILI (FRANCE)

This route follows a southwest-facing gully that is narrow and steep, with icefalls early in the season and rockfall danger later on. When Mesili

ALA DERECHA
FROM THE APPROACH
TO CABEZA DE CONDOR

GULLY 1/
MESILI ROUTE

GULLY 2 ROUTE

GULLY 3 ROUTE

GULLY 4/
COLIBRI ROUTE

ASTIER-GABARROU ROUTE

first climbed the route, access was easy via a snow ramp to the start of the route. The snow slope is now very steep rock.

Descent: From the top of the routes, continue left along a series of small rock peaks to reach the glaciated summit. Descend to join the Normal Route down from Cabeza de Condor.

GULLY 2

This route is believed to have been climbed, but I have no information on it.

GULLY 3

Grade III+/D, 60°, 400 m/1,300 ft

This route is the easiest of the four gullies, but it is still challenging. The route is mainly névé, but there are some ice sections.

Descent: See Gully 1

GULLY 4/COLIBRI ROUTE

Grade V/TD, 90°, 400 m/1,300 ft, 6 hours

SEPTEMBER 10, 1989, YVES ASTIER, YVAN ESTIENNE, AND PATRICK GABARROU (FRANCE)

The farthest left of the four gullies provides an excellent ice/mixed climb—when in good condition—that is steep, hard, and narrow. The climbing starts at 50°, steepens to 80° by the fifth pitch, and then hits 90° at about half way. At this point, go right and the angle slackens off to 60° and then 55° before reaching the ridge at 5,430 m/17,815 ft. Follow the ridge toward the left to the summit.

Descent: See Gully 1

ASTIER-GABARROU ROUTE

Grade V/TD, 80°, 400 m/1,300 ft

SEPTEMBER 12, 1989, YVES ASTIER AND PATRICK GABARROU (FRANCE)

The route starts at the base of Gully 4 but immediately heads left at 60° before reaching the central steep section of about 20 m/60 ft at 80°. The angle then relents to 55°, and the route continues up to

reach the ridge. During some years there are vertical ice pitches and
mixed sections.

Descent: See Gully 1

HUALLOMEN
(WYOMING)

5,463 m/17,923 ft

1964 (YUGOSLAVIA) FROM THE "BACK," WHICH IS NOW THE DESCENT ROUTE

This peak is a pretty evil-looking lump of rock with a number of steep
ice lines going up the southwest face, although only one has been climbed
so far. This route is the hardest one yet done in the Condoriri area.

Approach

From base camp, head up valley around the higher sedimented lake,
and then head left through moraine scree to join the glacier at its
tongue. Follow the glacier up and around to the right to get to the bottom of the face.

MESILI ROUTE

Grade V+ (5.9)/ ED1+ (VI), 85°, 400 m/1,300 ft, 8 hours

SEPTEMBER 15, 1976, ALAIN MESILI (FRANCE), SOLO

The sun never shines on this route, which is best done early in the season when there is more ice to climb and more snow to reach the bottom
of the climb. Because of glacial retreat, the route is considerably harder
than when Mesili did it. The right-hand snow gully is steeper (65°+) and
has vertical ice sections, but there is minimal rockfall danger compared
to the left-hand gully, which is pure snow. (When Mesili climbed the
route, there were no gullies, just a broad snowfield leading up to the start
of the route proper.)

From where the two lower gullies meet, head up and then go steeply
left (85°) to join a rising traverse that joins the ridge just below the summit. This section ends with 20 m/65 ft of loose rock (5.5/IV), which
brings you to the summit.

Descent: From the summit, head back east along the summit ridge,
and then descend off the back via rock ledges (5.3/II) down to the snow-
covered southeast face. Descend the face to the main glacier below, and
then go across to join the Pequeño Alpamayo Route down the glacier.

HUALLOMEN
FROM THE SOUTHWEST

MESILI ROUTE

HUALLOMEN
FROM THE SOUTHEAST

BRITISH ROUTE

BRITISH ROUTE

Grade V/TD+, 90°, 350 m/1,150 ft, 8 hours

JULY 31, 1997, STEVE RICHARDSON AND ANGUS RIDGE (U.K.)

Follow the Normal Route for Pequeño Alpamayo until you are below the southeast face of Huallomen. Head straight for the corner that drops down to the right of the summit. Cross the bergschrund and move up the slow slope that steepens from 60° to 65° to 70°. After 150 m/500 ft, reach a narrow rock band at 80°. Climb the rock and then another 80 m/260 ft of snow at 60° to 65° to arrive at the base of the obvious couloir. Climb the couloir with sections of 75° and 90° to reach the base of a narrower *goulotte*. British finish: Climb the goulotte directly to the cornice, which is passed on the left. If this is overhung by a snow and ice cornice, follow the Italian variant: go left up through mixed ground and a chimney (IV+) to reach the summit ridge.

Descent: Go off the back, and then descend to the col between Huallomen and Tarija. Join the Normal Route descending from Pequeño Alpamayo.

PEQUEÑO ALPAMAYO
(ALPAMAYO CHICO, FABULOSA)

5,370 m/17,618 ft

AUGUST 24, 1962, IRENE AND KEITH WHITELOCK (SOUTH AFRICA)

This peak is impressive, beautiful, and justifiably popular. From base camp, you can see only the top part of the summit, but the view of the mountain from Tarija is awesome. The pyramid of snow and rock looks much harder to climb than it is. The descent presents more problems than the ascent—either from crampons balling-up or from having to downclimb short ice sections.

Approach

From base camp, head up valley past the higher sedimented lake, and then go up to the right through boulder moraine to reach a moraine ridge made up of finer material. Head up the ridge, but turn off to the left before reaching the large boulder. Follow the path as it traverses before dropping to the glacier in 1½ hours from camp. Cross the flat part of the glacier to the other side, and then head up on the left-hand side of the glacier to reach the top. Go right and up to reach the minor

Nieve penitentes on the way to Pequeño Alpamayo, Cordillera Real

PEQUEÑO ALPAMAYO
FROM TARIJA

WEST-SOUTHWEST RIDGE
NORMAL ROUTE

DIRECTISIMA SOUTHEAST FACE ROUTE

summit of Tarija after 2 hours on the glacier. Descend 50 m/165 ft of loose rock (5.3/II) from the summit of Tarija to rejoin the snow below.

WEST–SOUTHWEST RIDGE NORMAL ROUTE

Grade III-/AD, 45-55°, 250 m/800 ft, 4 hours from base camp

AUGUST 24, 1962, IRENE AND KEITH WHITELOCK (SOUTH AFRICA)

Traverse the snow ridge to reach the Pequeño Alpamayo ridge, and then follow it to the summit in 1 hour. Keep a sensible distance away from the edge—much of it is in fact a cornice. During some seasons the Normal Route follows a rising traverse to the left from the base of the ridge. This is less steep than the ridge route but not as aesthetically pleasing.

Descent: Same

Moving up toward Pequeño Alpamayo, Cordillera Real

DIRECTISIMA SOUTHEAST FACE ROUTE

Grade III/D-, 55°, 250 m/800 ft, 1 hour from the col

1990 (U.S.)

When the West–Southwest Ridge starts to rise, traverse across the bottom of the face until below the summit. Climb the uniform slope straight to the summit, which is a loose snow nightmare early in the season and can be a névé dream later on.

Descent: Normal Route

PIRÁMIDE BLANCA

5,230 m/17,159 ft

1964 (YUGOSLAVIA)

The origins of the name for this mountain have been lost in the current age of glacial retreat, which has left the peak three-quarters rock and black rather than white. The Southwest Face routes are relatively short but interesting.

Approach

The approach is the same as for Pequeño Alpamayo (see above) until you reach the glacier. From the glacier, head up toward whatever part of the Southwest Face interests you, or head for the easy slopes leading up the Normal Route to the left of the rock part of Pirámide Blanca.

NORMAL ROUTE

Grade I/PD, 40°, 300 m/1,000 ft, 3 hours

Follow the glacier up to the left of the rock section of Pirámide Blanca, but stay below Diente and watch out for crevasses. Bear right and continue up until the snow eventually runs out and a short rock scramble (5.3/II) brings you to the summit.

Descent: Same

SOUTHWEST FACE/WEST RIDGE ROUTE

Grade II/AD, 60°, 200 m/650 ft, 4 hours

Climb rock slabs to the right of the mountain to reach the col in between Pirámide Blanca and Ilusioncita, and then follow the snow

PIRAMIDE BLANCA
FROM THE SOUTHWEST

SOUTHWEST FACE DIRECT ROUTE

SOUTHWEST FACE/
WEST RIDGE ROUTE

NORMAL ROUTE

ridge toward the left to the rock summit. The exact line depends on snow conditions; take care if there is a cornice above.

Descent: Normal Route

SOUTHWEST FACE DIRECT ROUTE

Grade III/D-, 80°, 200 m/650 ft, 4 hours

AUGUST 1988, GEOFFREY BARTRAM, DAVID PELTIER, AND NEVIN WHITELAW (U.S.)

This route follows the most direct line on the mountain. If the ice curtain has formed, head up the snow and rock triangle to reach the base of the 4 m/13 ft ice section. If the ice section has not formed, pass this section to the left or right, and then head straight up the face to reach the ridge to the right (east) of the summit.

Descent: Normal Route

ILUSIONCITA

5,150 m/16,896 ft

SEPTEMBER 1, 1962, A. GONZÁLEZ, ALFREDO MARTÍNEZ (BOLIVIA),
AND KEITH WHITELOCK (SOUTH AFRICA)

Literally known as "Little Ilusión" in comparison to its larger southern neighbor, Ilusión, Ilusioncita offers one short route that provides the opportunity for a lot of practice on how to weave a way through a broken glacier.

Approach

The approach is the same as for Pequeño Alpamayo (see above) until you reach the turnoff from the moraine ridge. Instead of turning off to the left, carry on up and then work a way toward the right to the left-hand side of the glacier.

BOLIVIAN-SOUTH AFRICAN ROUTE

Grade II/AD-, 40°, 350 m/1,150 ft, 4 hours

Head up the glacier that descends from Ilusioncita and Ilusión to the left-hand side of the col between the two mountains. From the col, head

ILUSIONCITA AND ILUSION
FROM THE WEST

ILUSIONCITA

ILUSION

ILUSION DIRECT ROUTE

ILUSION NORMAL ROUTE

BOLIVIAN-SOUTH AFRICAN ROUTE

up left through a short rock section (5.3/II) to join the snow ridge, and follow it to the summit.

Descent: Same

***

ILUSIÓN

5,330 m/17,487 ft

SEPTEMBER 6, 1962, A. GONZÁLEZ, ALFREDO MARTÍNEZ (BOLIVIA),
IRENE AND KEITH WHITELOCK (SOUTH AFRICA)

Reasonably difficult routefinding on the Normal Route and short steep rock sections on the Direct Route make Ilusión a short but enjoyable challenge.

Approach

The approach is the same as for Ilusioncita (see above).

NORMAL ROUTE

Grade II (5.5)/AD (III), 40° (70°), 400 m/1,300 ft, 4 hours

Head up the broken glacier between Ilusión and Ilusioncita to the right-hand side of the col between the two mountains. Head up to the right, and scramble up the steep rock to reach the scree-covered slopes above. Move across toward the right to join the higher glacier sooner rather than later, and work a way up to the summit.

Descent: Same

DIRECT ROUTE

Grade III (5.5)/AD+ (III), 50° (70°), 400 m/1,300 ft, 4 hours

This route is steeper than the Normal Route and has more rock climbing, but it is aesthetically more pleasing than the easier route. From the bottom of the moraine ridge on the way to Pequeño Alpamayo, head off toward the right across scree to reach the cleaner and steeper rock. Climb through the rock section, taking the most direct line possible to reach the glacier above. Staying to the left of the seracs above, move up the glacier to reach the summit ridge, and follow it to the scree-covered flat summit.

Descent: Normal Route

Serac collapse and avalanche above Campamento Argentino on Huayna Potosí, Cordillera Real (Photo by Dr. Fran Shekelton)

HUAYNA POTOSÍ
(CACA ACA)
6,088 m/19,974 ft
MAY 1919, RUDOLF DIENST AND ADOLF SCHULZE (GERMANY)

Maps: IGM Milluni 5945 II, Walter Guzmán Córdova Huayna Potosí

Although describing Huayna Potosí as "the easiest '6000er' in the world" ignores its high-altitude challenge, there can be few mountains of this size that are more easily accessible: a jeep trip takes less than 2 hours to reach the base of the mountain from central La Paz. Seen from the Altiplano, the mountain is an imposing ice pyramid. The view changes from Zongo Pass, where it is possible to see the whole East Face, and the mountain becomes far more elongated and complicated.

Note: Remember to take your passport with you for the pointless but police-manned checkpoint at Milluni.

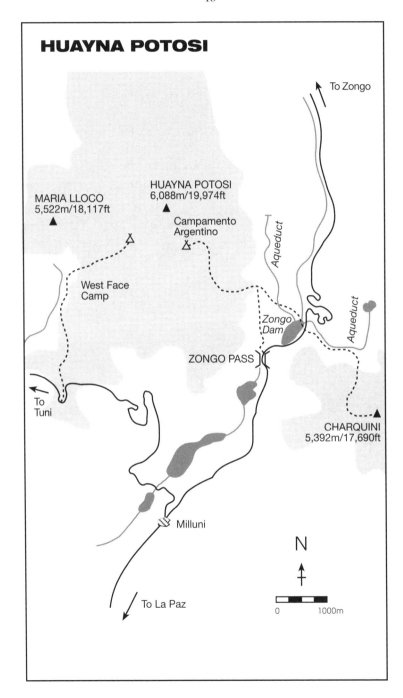

HUAYNA POTOSI

To Zongo

MARIA LLOCO
5,522m/18,117ft
▲

HUAYNA POTOSI
6,088m/19,974ft
▲

Campamento
Argentino

Aqueduct

West Face
Camp

Aqueduct

Zongo
Dam

ZONGO PASS

CHARQUINI
5,392m/17,690ft
▲

To
Tuni

Milluni

N
┼

0   1000m

To La Paz

Access to the East Face

The new approach is from the pass, marked by a cross, before reaching the Zongo dam. Camping is possible; ask the inhabitants of the white house up left from the road.

The old approach is from the wall of the Zongo dam. The hut next to the dam is not continually staffed but can be booked by ringing Refugio Huayna Potosí (La Paz 323584). It costs US$10 per night to stay;

Looking east from the Vía de los Franceses, Huayna Potosí, Cordillera Real

meals are extra. There is no legal, moral, or practical purpose to registering with the refuge. The notice misleadingly suggests that if you register at the refuge and then fail to return, someone will go to look for you. This is not the case.

A telephone at the pass is available for emergency use only. It is the property of the electricity-generation company Cobee. Speak to the dam guardian if you need to use it.

A jeep from La Paz to Zongo Pass costs US$75, and the trip takes less than 2 hours. Trucks and minibuses leave at regularly irregular intervals from Plaza Ballivían in El Alto (the area of La Paz around the airport). It is possible to hire a minibus from Plaza Ballivían for about US$10: arrive and haggle with drivers of empty minibuses.

To return from Huayna Potosí, arrange for a jeep to arrive at Zongo Pass at about 4:00 P.M. or be prepared to hang around waiting for passing vehicles with space.

Porters can be arranged to carry kit to Campamento Argentino at US$10 per porter, but hire only porters who have crampons and glacier glasses. If you want porters, contact the inhabitants of the white house at the pass or one of the specialist agencies in La Paz.

Approach

The new approach: from the pass, head up through rock and moraine to reach the obvious moraine ridge. Follow the ridge up, reaching its end in 1 hour from the pass. Drop down to the right before climbing a scree slope. At the top of the first scree slope, bear left to reach a level area of scree before continuing up and toward the left across more scree, and then up again to reach the edge of the glacier in under 1 hour. Cairns mark the route to the glacier.

The old approach: cross the dam wall, follow the aqueduct for 15 minutes, cross the aqueduct, and follow the well-defined path as it heads up to the base of the obvious moraine ridge. The route is then the same as the new approach.

The glacier gets less steep as you go up. Stay to the left of the rock spur, and continue up to a low ridge. Cross the ridge, and follow the normally well-defined path as it rises gently up and to the right. The path then turns to the left and becomes steep immediately before your arrival at Campamento Argentino (5,450 m/17,880 ft) after less than 2 hours on the glacier.

Take care at the Campamento Argentino high camp, especially

during the later part of the season when major crevasses open up to the left of the normal path. Camp and stay to the right of the path.

Do not camp below the serac-threatened wall to the right of the south summit. Some very large serac collapses have occurred there.

NORMAL ROUTE

Grade II/AD-, 50°, 600 m/1,950 ft, 4–6 hours

From Campamento Argentino, head up the glacier toward the East Face. Earlier in the season, continue up for 400 m/1,300 ft, and then turn right to join the ridge above. Later in the season, a bergschrund often opens up, and it is necessary to turn right 150 m/500 ft beyond the camp and head up to the ridge. Turn left, and then join the exposed La Pala, or Polish, ridge with 200 m/650 ft of 40° to 50° terrain. Cross a series of slopes and crevasses, and then traverse to arrive below the summit face after 3 hours.

There are two alternatives to the summit from this point: (1) go straight up the face for 250 m/800 ft at 40° to 50°; or (2) continue following the path toward the right until it reaches the ridge, and then go left and follow the airy ridge to the summit.

Both alternatives normally take 1 to 2 hours. The face route is easier to protect and is a better choice in windy conditions and toward the end of the season when snow and ice cover on the ridge can become thin. The ridge route gives impressive views down the 1,000 m/3,300 ft West Face and is not as steep as the more direct route.

Descent: You can descend via the face or the ridge. Campamento Argentino can be reached in 2 hours from the summit, and it takes another 2 hours down to the road.

VÍA DE LOS FRANCESES

Grade III/AD+, 55°, 300 m/1,000 ft, 3–4 hours from Campamento Argentino

AUGUST 12, 1974, THIERRY CARDON AND ALAIN MESILI (FRANCE)

From Campamento Argentino, head up toward the East Face. Before the Normal Route bears right, go left and work a route across the glacier toward the obvious line of the Vía de los Franceses, watching out for some very large crevasses on the way. In good conditions it is possible to reach the bergschrund in under 2 hours.

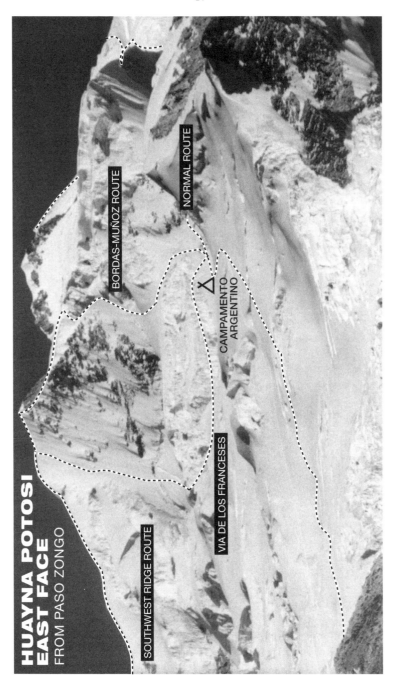

HUAYNA POTOSI EAST FACE FROM PASO ZONGO

BORDAS-MUÑOZ ROUTE

NORMAL ROUTE

CAMPAMENTO ARGENTINO

VIA DE LOS FRANCESES

SOUTHWEST RIDGE ROUTE

The route angles at 50°, and it is steeper at the top. Route time depends on conditions: climbing unconsolidated snow earlier in the season can take up to 4 hours, for example; however, after the snow has turned to ice, the route can be climbed considerably quicker, for example, in 38 minutes.

Descent: From the top, it is possible to traverse toward the right to the south summit, which is exhilarating and exposed (III/AD+), or drop down to the col between the north and south summits. It is also possible to traverse up to the north, principal, summit above the West Face, which is very exposed (III+/D-), but be extremely careful later in the season after the snow has turned to ice. Alternatively, you can drop down toward the left to join the Normal Route below the summit face.

BORDAS-MUÑOZ ROUTE
Grade III/AD+, 75°, 300 m/1,000 ft, 8 hours

JULY 19, 1990, ELISA GONZÁLEZ, JULIÁN HEVIA, ENRIQUE REY,
AND JUAN CARLOS VÁZQUEZ (SPAIN)

From Campamento Argentino, head straight for the East Face, aiming for the right-hand side of the rock outcrop. Follow a snow ramp

Downclimbing a rocky section on the southwest ridge of Huayna Potosí, Cordillera Real (Photo by Jason Currie)

up, and then traverse across the face before climbing up to the south summit ridge and continuing to the summit. The options from the summit are the same as those described for Vía de los Franceses above.

Descent: Normal Route

SOUTHWEST RIDGE ROUTE

Grade II/AD, 50°, 800 m/2,600 ft, 10 hours

AUGUST 3–6, 1963, PAUL BARKER (U.S.) AND FRED HENDEL (AUSTRIA)

This superb but long route follows the exposed Southwest Ridge, crossing three small summits to reach the south summit. It is possible to start the route at its geographically logical start in the Milluni valley (which is what Barker and Hendel did), but this makes for a very long route.

Alternatively, camp at Campamento Argentino, and head left across the glacier to reach the ridge, or camp below the ridge. The route can sometimes have long sections of soft snow, and there are cornices and crevasses to negotiate.

Descent: Normal Route

■ ■ ■

Access for the West Face

The 1,000 m/3,300 ft West Face of Huayna Potosí is the biggest face in Bolivia. Most of its routes present a stamina test rather than a technical challenge. The face averages 55°, although most routes have steep pitches up to 70°. Unless you and your partner are confident and going strongly, it is worth carrying bivouac gear on West Face routes because of the high incidence of unplanned bivouacs, often on the face itself or during the descent.

Climbing times vary depending on snow conditions, fitness, and the route selected; for example, routes have been climbed in 4 to 18 hours. After the snow turns to ice, normally during June, West Face routes take longer, and there is a greater threat of serac falls.

No public transportation is available to the West Face area. Hire a jeep for the trip from La Paz, turning off the road to the Zongo Pass at Milluni and then following the road toward Tuni. When the jeep reaches the highest point after climbing out of the Milluni valley, get out. Travel by jeep takes 2 hours from La Paz and costs US$75.

Approach

The joy of the walk-in to the West Face is that it is downhill to the glacier from the road and then a gentle 2-hour stroll up the glacier. Routefinding is not a problem: from the bivouac site, pick a line and go.

Descent for all West Face routes: Normal Route via the East Face. An alternative, descended by Jason Currie and Mark Ryle (U.K.) in 1996, is to follow the Southwest Ridge down from the south summit until it becomes relatively easy to drop down to the flat glacier at the bottom of the West Face. The advantage of the Currie-Ryle descent is that you end up returning to your bivouac gear at the bottom of the West Face instead of having to walk around the mountain from the Zongo Pass or

carrying all your kit up the route with you. However, the ridge is not always in good condition.

LABA-HUDSON ROUTE (VÍA AMERICA)
Grade IV (5.5)/D+ (IV+), 80°, 1,000 m/3,300 ft, 12 hours
JULY 4–5, 1969, JOHN HUDSON AND ROMAN LABA (U.S.)

This route was the first one climbed on the West Face. From the bivouac site, take the easiest line up to the mixed west (left) ridge line. Follow the ridge line to its junction with the Northwest Ridge and then onto the summit.

AMERICAN ROUTE
(Later named VÍA DE LYON
by French climbers unaware of the previous ascent)
Grade IV-/D-, 65°, 1,000 m/3,300 ft, 4–18 hours
JULY 1970, DOBBS HARTHORNE, ANDY HARVARD, JAMES LANNEY,
AND TODD THOMPSON (U.S.)

The first route climbed on the actual face took the North Americans 2 days and is now the most popular route on the face, although every party appears to do a slight variation. Go up the left-hand side of the huge hanging glacier, traverse toward the right over the top of it, and then continue across to reach a gully. (Some people cross below the hanging glacier and then head up.) Continue up the gully to reach the summit ridge 20 m/65 ft to the right (south) of the summit.

YUGOSLAV ROUTE
Grade IV/D+, 70°, 1,000 m/3,300 ft, 12 hours
JUNE 14, 1983, BLAZ JEREB AND MIRKO POGACAR (SLOVENIA)

This is an elegant and direct route up the face. Climb up the left-hand side of the large hanging glacier (50°). Where the American Route turns right to cross the hanging glacier, continue straight up through two ice pitches, and stay to the right of the rock wall for as long as possible. The rock wall is climbed via an icefall (70°) coming down from the summit

Ice formations on the West Face of Huayna Potosí, Cordillera Real

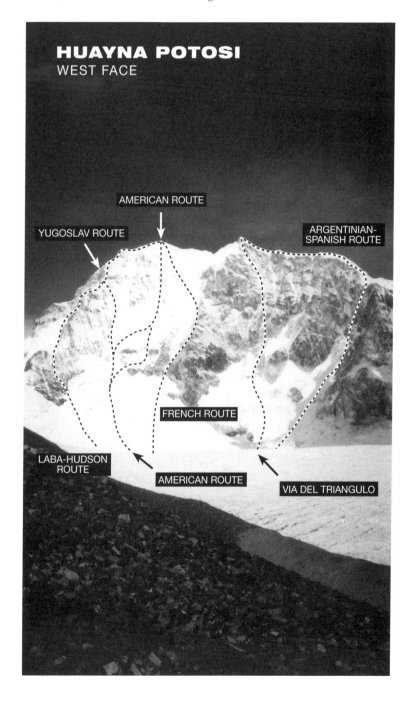

HUAYNA POTOSI
WEST FACE

AMERICAN ROUTE

YUGOSLAV ROUTE

ARGENTINIAN-
SPANISH ROUTE

FRENCH ROUTE

LABA-HUDSON
ROUTE

AMERICAN ROUTE

VIA DEL TRIANGULO

Looking across at storm clouds over the Yungas from Huayna Potosí,
Cordillera Real

ridge. The route finishes up on iced or verglassed rock (60°) to reach
the summit ridge. Turn right on the ridge, and continue to the summit.

FRENCH ROUTE

Grade IV/D, 70°, 1,000 m/3,300 ft

APRIL 1978, JEAN AND MICHEL AFFANASIEF (FRANCE)

Climb up to the right of the hanging glacier, and then follow the snow
gully to the left of the rock outcrop until a line to the summit becomes
clear. The route reaches the summit ridge slightly to the right of the
summit.

VÍA DEL TRIANGULO

Grade IV (5.5)/D- (IV), 70°, 800 m/2,600 ft

SEPTEMBER 18, 1971, HANS HAZTLER (AUSTRIA–GERMANY) AND ALAIN MESILI (FRANCE)

Climb up the snowfields directly below the south summit. Then work
a way up the mixed gully above, which curves around to the left, to reach
the south summit. The route becomes steeper and harder the higher
you get.

On the way down the Huayna Potosí Normal Route looking south, Cordillera Real

ARGENTINIAN-SPANISH ROUTE

Grade IV/D+, 80°, 1,000 m/3,300 ft

1990, CAROLINA AND HORACIO GODÓ, MARCELO PAGANI (ARGENTINA),
AND ALVARO ENRIQUEZ (SPAIN)

Follow the snow as far to the right and up as it will go before heading up a sometimes mixed section. Follow this section to join the Southwest Ridge, and then take the ridge to the south summit. The traverse can be continued above the West Face to reach the main, north summit.

NORTH-SOUTH TRAVERSE

Grade III/AD+, 70°, 1,000 m/3,300 ft, 3 days

JUNE 24–27, 1993, SIMON ABRAHAMS, JIM HALL, AND TONY MATTHEWS (U.K.)

To climb this route, start on the north ridge, move across to the west flank, and continue across to the northwest ridge to meet the snow line. Follow the northwest ridge with mixed climbing over rock (5.5/IV) and ice (55°) to the Normal Route, 200 m/650 ft below the summit. From the summit, continue south to the south summit (70° snow/ice), and then descend the ridge until an easy descent to Campamento Argentino becomes clear. Descend to the camp, and follow the Normal Route back to Zongo Pass.

southern section
of the cordillera real

This section stretches from La Cumbre, the main pass crossing the Bolivian Andes, to the Río La Paz or Río Abajo that cuts through the Andes dividing it into the Cordilleras Real and Quimsa Cruz. At this point the Andes are made up of a series of small ranges and then the large lumps of Mururata and Illimani, the end marker of the range.

HATI KHOLLU

5,421 m/17,785 ft

Map: IGM CHOJLLA 6044 IV

The Hampaturi Group is clearly visible from the Sopocachi area of La Paz, and it contains the closest glaciers to the city. However, it is rarely visited by climbers, and the area is sparsely populated despite being so close. Hati Khollu is the highest peak in the small range, and from its summit you have great views of Mururata and Illimani. The climb provides a pleasant way to acclimatize.

Access

From the center of La Paz, take a bus to the suburb of Alto Pampahasi. About 100m/330 ft before the end of the asphalt there is a side street on the left, from where buses go to Palcoma (marked "Estancia Karpani" on the IGM map). The trip takes 45 minutes and costs US$1. Alternatively, haggle with a driver of an empty minibus to hire the whole bus for about US$7.

A jeep trip from La Paz to Palcoma takes 1 hour and costs US$30.

Approach

From Palcoma at 3,850 m/12,630 ft, cross the river and head up the valley that comes down from the east. Go up the valley, staying on the right-hand side. At the point where the rarely used vehicle track ends, cross the stream, and follow llama paths up and to the left. Cross another stream, and follow the obvious contour path up and to the left below the pointed rock peak. Stay on the left-hand side of the stream until you reach Laguna Jachcha Khasiri at 4,690 m/15,387 ft. Camp at the far end of the lake, 4 hours from Palcoma.

SOUTHWEST FACE/SOUTHEAST RIDGE ROUTE

Grade III- (5.3)/AD (II), 60°, 400 m/1,300 ft, 3 hours

MAY 15, 1995, YOSSI BRAIN (U.K.) AND JASON DAVIS (U.S.)

From the lake, head up the valley to join the flat part of the glacier. Cross the glacier, and then take the steepest and most direct line up to the ridge. Follow the ridge to just below the summit where a gully made up of easy-angled loose rock leads to the summit.

Descent: Same to the ridge and then follow the ridge down until easier angled slopes lead back down to the right to the flat glacier.

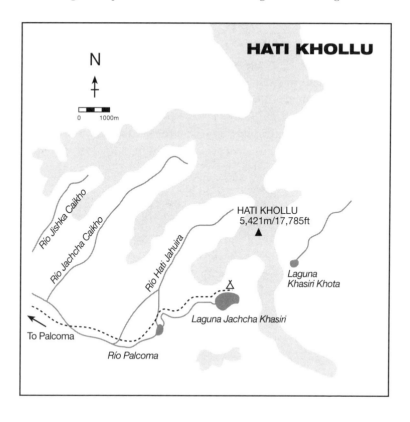

HATI KHOLLU
FROM LAGUNA JACHCHA KHASIRI

SOUTHWEST FACE/
SOUTHEAST RIDGE ROUTE

Chola porters on the way up to Nido de Condores, Illimani, Cordillera Real

■ ■ ■

ILLIMANI

6,439 m/21,125 ft

SEPTEMBER 9, 1898, SIR MARTIN CONWAY (U.K.), JEAN-ANTOINE MAQUIGNAZ,
AND LUIGI PELISIER (SWISS-ITALIAN) FROM THE SOUTHEAST

Maps: DAV CORDILLERA REAL-SÜD (ILLIMANI), IGM PALCA 6044 III AND COHONI 6043 IV,
AND WALTER GUZMÁN CÓRDOVA ILLIMANI

Illimani is the highest and southernmost peak in the Cordillera Real
and dominates views from the capital city of La Paz. Hans Ertl, writing
in *Mountain World* (1953), described Illimani as "one of the most beautiful and impressive groups of peaks in South America." It is not so much
a mountain as a massif—the glaciation measures 8 km/5 mi from one
end to the other. From La Paz, the mountain appears to have three summits: the highest, Pico Sur, is to the right, but two other major summits
are hidden from view, as well as a number of others. The west side is

heavily glaciated, while the rarely climbed south and east sides present imposing ice gullies.

Access and Approach via Estancia Una and Pinaya

Day 1: Although Illimani appears to be just at the end of a number of streets in La Paz, the journey by jeep to Estancia Una or Pinaya takes more than 2 hours and costs US$160. Both Estancia Una and Pinaya have a good supply of mules and porters waiting to be hired.

A bus often goes to Quilihuaya, a village located a couple of hours' walk from Estancia Una. It leaves at 5:00 A.M. from near the Comedor Popular on Calle Max Paredes in the Rodríguez market area of La Paz. The bus sometimes continues up to the aqueduct below Estancia Una, which cuts the walk to the village to 30 minutes. Mules from Una cost US$8 for the 3-hour walk to first camp at Puente Roto (4,400 m/14,440 ft).

From Una, follow the road up valley to Pinaya. The road is drivable to Pinaya, thereby saving the first hour's walk out of Una. From the school in Pinaya at the end of the road it is only 1½ hour's walk to Puente Roto. Mules cost US$6.

From Pinaya, follow paths through the houses and farms toward the long west face of Illimani and then cross a series of steppes to arrive at a large flat area crossed by streams below an unused mining road. This is an excellent campsite with views of the central and south summits of Illimani, of Huayna Potosí, and also the lights of La Paz.

Access and Approach via Cohoni

Day 1 (alternate): Buses are available at the corner of Calle General Luis Lara and Calle Boqueron, San Pedro district, for the trip from La Paz to Cohoni on Monday through Saturday at 1:00 P.M. and 3:00 P.M. The journey takes 4 hours and costs US$2. The return journey to La Paz leaves Cohoni on Monday through Saturday at 2:00 A.M.

From Cohoni square (3,530 m/11,580 ft), follow the road down and out as it heads back toward La Paz. Five minutes down the road a broad, roughly paved path leads up to the right—follow it. After ½ hour, a notch through a ridge leads to a view of most of the west side of Illimani. Continue on up the path, staying to the right of the Río Huacanasca and eventually joining it. Carry on until you arrive at Puente Roto (4,400 m/14,440 ft).

Day 2: From Puente Roto, follow the mining road for 15 minutes, and then head up to the left, aiming for a scree slope that leads to the rock ridge coming down from below Pico Sur. Head up and join the ridge,

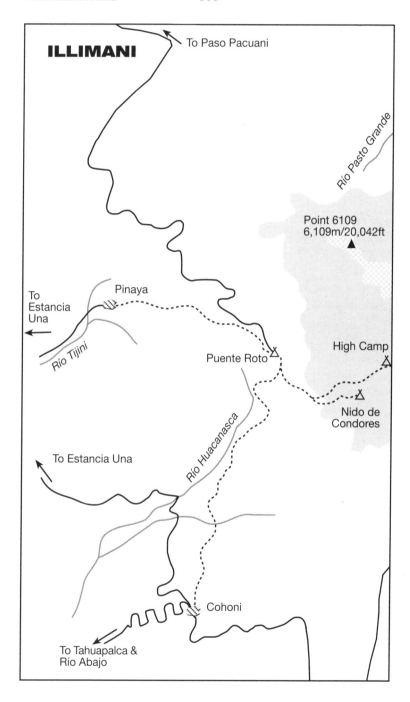

ILLIMANI

To Paso Pacuani

Río Pasto Grande

Point 6109
6,109m/20,042ft
▲

Pinaya

To
Estancia
Una

Río Tijini

Puente Roto

High Camp

Nido de
Condores

To Estancia Una

Río Huacanasca

Cohoni

To Tahuapalca &
Río Abajo

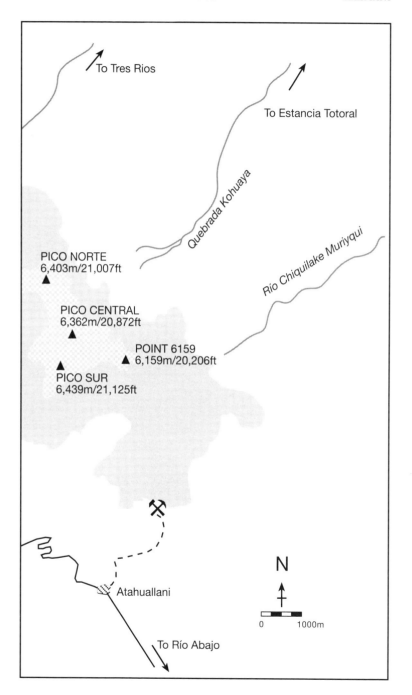

and follow it to reach the high camp of Nido de Condores (literally, "the condors' nest") for Pico Sur in 4 to 6 hours. The camp (5,450 m/17,880 ft) is normally a flat rocky platform next to a glacier, but after a bad wet season it can be snow-covered. There is often no running water, and it is necessary to melt snow. Porters can be arranged from Puente Roto to Nido de Condores and for the descent (US$10 per porter). Pico Norte routes start from a different high camp (below).

PICO SUR

6,439 m/21,125 ft

From La Paz, Pico Sur is the right hand of the three obvious peaks, and is the highest peak on the mountain. Rather conveniently, Pico Sur's normal route is the easiest route on the mountain, and it gets you to its highest point.

NORMAL ROUTE

Grade II/PD, 50°, 1,000 m/3,300 ft, 5–7 hours

MARCH 22–23, 1940, ROLF BOETTGER, FRIEDRICH FRITZ, AND WILFRID KÜHM (GERMANY)

From the Nido de Condores camp, follow the ridge which rises steeply. Be careful—six Chileans fell to their deaths descending this section in 1989. Some very large crevasses are found on the route, but these are normally clear, and it is just a matter of working a way around them. The steepest section of the route (50°) is 20 m/65 ft long and is snow during the early part of the season and often ice later on. Aim for the notch to the north (left) of the summit; go through the notch, and head toward the right. Unfortunately, the summit in front of you is not the true summit. Climb the false summit, and follow the long, airy ridge to reach the highest point at the far (southern) end.

The climb is very cold because the sun rises on the opposite side of the mountain. As a result, the west face does not receive any sun before 9:00 A.M. Unfortunately, because of the length of the climb, it is necessary to start from Nido de Condores around 4:00 A.M. to be safely and quickly down before the snow softens in the sun.

Descent: The same, but a lot faster. The descent takes 2 to 3 hours from the summit to Nido de Condores and another 2 to 3 hours to Puente Roto.

Moving up Illimani's northeast ridge with Mururata in the background,
Cordillera Real

ILLIMANI PICO SUR
FROM PUENTE ROTO

NIDO DE CONDORES

NORMAL ROUTE

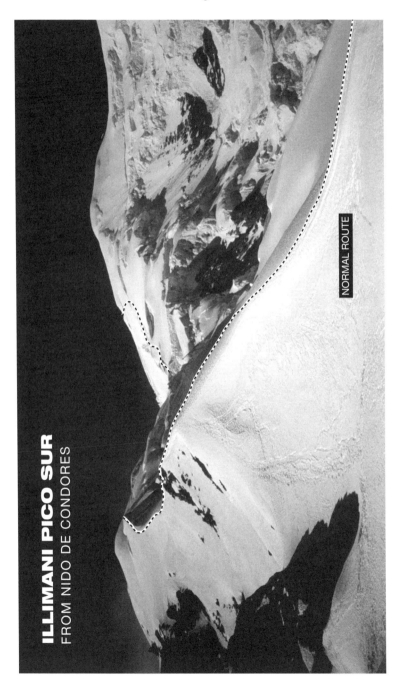

ILLIMANI PICO SUR
FROM NIDO DE CONDORES

NORMAL ROUTE

ILLIMANI PICO SUR

FROM FLAT SECTION APPROX. 5,800m/19,000ft

NORMAL ROUTE

PICO NORTE

6,403 m/21,007 ft

MAY 6, 1950, HANS ERTL AND GERT SCHRÖDER (GERMANY)

From La Paz, Pico Norte is the left-hand of the three obvious peaks. Some of the most impressive climbing on Illimani is found on Pico Norte, and Ertl and Schröder's route—the first on the peak—was the hardest route climbed in Bolivia to that date.

GERMAN ROUTE (SOUTH RIDGE)

Grade III/D-, 70°, 1,000 m/3,300 ft, 12 hours

MAY 6, 1950, HANS ERTL AND GERT SCHRÖDER (GERMANY)

From the Nido de Condores high camp at 5,450 m/17,880 ft (see Pico Sur above), follow the Normal Route until you reach the flat section at approx. 5,800 m/19,000 ft. Instead of continuing up the normal route, drop left 200 m/650 ft to reach the glacial basin below. Cross the basin to arrive at the lowest point of Pico Norte's south ridge to the left (north) of the small subsidiary peak on the ridge between Picos Norte and Central. Climb straight up to join the ridge (60–70° depending on snow conditions), turn left and continue along the beautifully exposed ridge—the drop to the right down the east face is 1,000 m/3,300 ft. About 200 m/650 ft below the summit there is often a crevasse and a 50 m/165 ft ice cliff. At the base of the cliff, traverse right off the ridge, cross the crevasse to reach the slope, and then climb this direct (60°) to rejoin the ridge and follow it to the summit.

Descent: Same or follow the west ridge of Pico Norte down until you reach its lowest point. Drop down left to reach the glacial basin below. Cross the basin and rejoin your footsteps coming down from the flat section on the Pico Sur normal route.

VÍA DEL INDIO

Grade III/D-, 50°, 300 m/1,000 ft

To reach the bottom of the route, follow the description for the German Route above. After crossing the glacial basin, arrive directly below the face coming down directly from Pico Norte. The route heads straight up the face to join Pico Norte's south ridge. Either descend the south

ILLIMANI PICO NORTE
FROM NIDO DE CONDORES RIDGE

GERMAN ROUTE (SOUTH RIDGE)

VIA DEL INDIO

VIA KHOYA KHOYU

LEFT-HAND ALTERNATIVE ROUTE

ridge or continue up it (see German Route description above).

Descent: See German Route above.

VÍA KHOYA KHOYU

Grade III/D-, 60°, 350 m/1,150 ft

JULY 25-27, 1972, ALAIN MESILI (FRANCE) AND ERNESTO SÁNCHEZ (BOLIVIA)

Aesthetically, this is one of the most beautiful routes on the mountain. From Puente Roto, follow the mining road as if you were going up to Nido de Condores, but turn off to the left after crossing the stream. Work a way up through scree and rock to reach the glacier that comes down between Picos Central and Norte.

From a bivouac below the face, climb immediately to the left of the rocks through 60° ice to reach the face. Stay on the right-hand edge of the face to reach Pico Norte's west ridge and follow it to Pico Norte.

Descent: Retrace your steps until you are at the base of Pico Norte's west ridge again, then descend right to arrive at the glacial basin near the start of the route.

LEFT-HAND ALTERNATIVE ROUTE

Grade III/D-, 60°, 350 m/1,150 ft

This is the route preferred by climbers starting from Puente Roto who are not eager to bivouac below the face. From Puente Roto, head up through scree and then rock to join the glacier below the distinctive pyramidal face. Climb the face via the left-hand side to join the ridge above. From this point the route is the same as for the Vía Khoya Khoyu.

Descent: See Vía Khoya Khoyu above.

ILLIMANI TRAVERSES

The three main peaks of Illimani (Norte, Central, and Sur) have been linked in a traverse a number of times. The five-peak traverse has been done twice. For either traverse, complete acclimatization is essential, as are supreme fitness and the ability to spend a minimum of three nights at or above 6,000 m/20,000 ft. The grades given are technical; it is impossible to take into account the effects of successive days of climbing with full rucksacks and sleeping at high altitude.

THREE-PEAK TRAVERSE

Grade III/D-, 70°, 2,000 m/6,500 ft, 8 km/5 mi, 4-6 days

AUGUST 1957, WERNER KARL, HANS RICHTER, AND HANS WIMMER (GERMANY)

From Puente Roto, climb Pico Norte by the Vía Khoya Khoyu or the Left-Hand Alternative Route (see above). Descend Pico Norte's south ridge. A good bivouac site is on the eastern side of the ridge at its lowest point before the minor peak. Climb Pico Central's north ridge. Descend to a possible camp in the col between the Picos Central and Sur. Climb Pico Sur and then descend the normal route to Nido de Condores and then carry on down back to Puente Roto.

FIVE-PEAK TRAVERSE

Grade III/D-, 70°, 2,000 m/6,500 ft, 16 km/10 mi, 5+ days

SOUTH-NORTH AUGUST 19-23, 1979, ANTON AND RIA PUTZ (GERMANY)

NORTH-SOUTH AUGUST 25-29, 1998, YOSSI BRAIN, PETER GROSSET (U.K.), ALESSANDRO BIANCHI, AND MARCELLO SANGUINETI (ITALY)

This is the longest and most impressive mountaineering expedition in Bolivia. The route is described from north to south because if you hire a jeep to get in, you save 1,000 m/3,300 ft of ascent.

Hire a jeep from La Paz. Follow the road toward Tres Rios but take the right-hand turning at Point 4460 on the DAV map, which is shortly before the high point of the road, Paso Pacuani. Follow the road and, immediately after crossing the Río Umabamba, turn up left and follow the road as far as possible toward Mina Aguila. The road is washed out at approx. 4,450 m/14,600 ft.

Follow the valley up, past Mina Aguila, to its end. Turn right and cross the boulder scree to reach the edge of the glacier at approx. 5,400 m/ 17,700 ft and camp.

Join the glacier and head up to join Illimani's north ridge. Follow the ridge up and over the as-marked Pico del Indio (Point 6109) and continue until you reach a bivouac site immediately after the overhanging ice structure of Point 6175.

Continue following the ridge. Climb Pico Norte, then descend Pico Norte's south ridge to reach a good bivouac site on the eastern (left-hand) side of the ridge immediately before the minor peak.

Climb Pico Central by its north ridge. Drop down to the broad basin between Picos Central and Sur to camp.

Climb Pico Sur and then descend the broad basin to reach the as-marked Pico Layca Khollu (Point 6159). From the last peak, drop down to the glacier below and follow this down until its end. Depending on conditions, descend snow or rock gullies to reach the scree slopes below. Follow these down to an abandoned mining camp at approx. 4,400 m/ 14,400 ft.

From the mining camp, follow paths down to and then along the aqueduct, then through cultivated fields, aiming to join the road near Atahuallani at Point 3693. Follow the road to Cohoni from where there is a daily bus service to La Paz at 2:00 A.M.

CHAPTER 5

cordillera quimsa cruz

I am a yob. Thus the height of aesthetic achievement is to drive to the

foot of the cliff and overcome the crux by trampolining off the seat of

one's motorcycle. . . . Imagine then my delight in finding a virgin

peak where it was not only possible to drive to a base camp but to

actually don crampons in the relative comfort of a Land Rover and

from there to step directly onto firm Andean snow.

Roger Whewell, "A Yob's-Eye View of the Quimsa Cruz"
American Alpine Journal, 1968–69

this range is the smallest, lowest, and least visited of Bolivia's four major cordilleras, through no fault of its own. Adrián Aponte described the area in the *American Alpine Journal* (1964–65) as "An infinite number of nameless peaks of incomparable beauty," while Evelio Echevarría described the range in *Pyrenaica* (no. 162, 1991) as "A South American Karakoram." The Quimsa Cruz, sometimes called the Tres Cruces (Three Crosses), has around 80 peaks in the 4,900 to 5,800 m/16,000 to 19,000 ft range. The lack of 6,000 m/20,000 ft peaks means the Quimsa Cruz has

Gigante Grande and Laguna Laram Khota from the Viloco road,
Quimsa Cruz

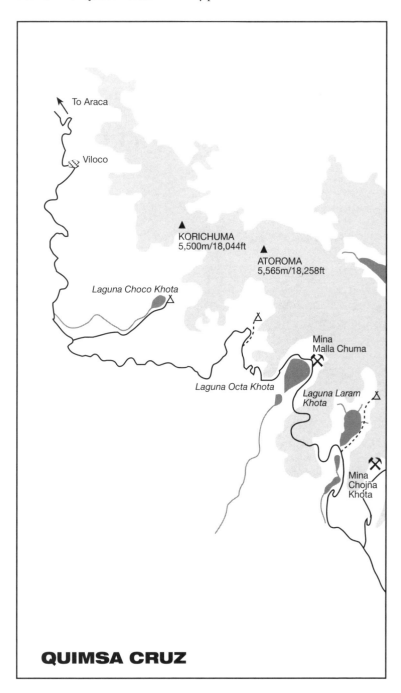

To Araca

Viloco

KORICHUMA
5,500m/18,044ft

ATOROMA
5,565m/18,258ft

Laguna Choco Khota

Mina
Malla Chuma

Laguna Octa Khota

Laguna Laram
Khota

Mina
Chojña
Khota

QUIMSA CRUZ

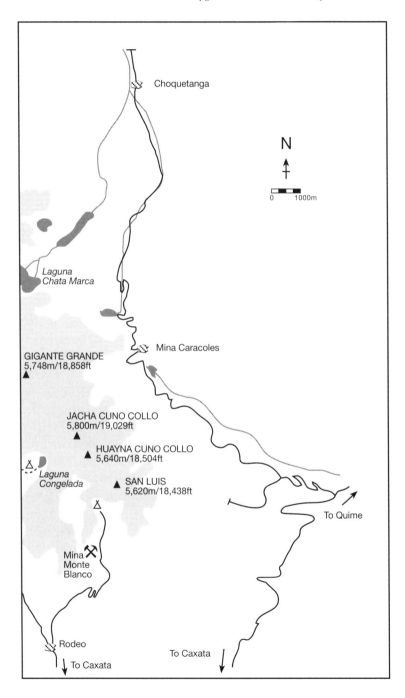

rarely been visited by major peak-bagging expeditions, so it offers the greatest opportunity for new routes. The north is predominantly an area for rock climbing on granodiorite spires, likened to the Chamonix aiguilles by a number of climbers. The snow peaks are in the southern part of the range and not very far away. The entire range is 40 km/25 mi long and less than 15 km/9 mi wide, and it is well-served by mining roads, buses, and trucks carrying around miners that can easily get to 4,500 m/14,750 ft. Access is easy as long as you are willing to hire a jeep or work out the public transportation options, or are prepared to hang around. Most base camps provide a base for a number of peaks, so you can get in 4 or 5 days of climbing without having to break camp.

Note: There is more confusion over names and heights in the Quimsa Cruz than in any other area of Bolivia.

ACCESS

The route to Viloco from La Paz follows the La Paz–Oruro road as far as Khonani where you turn left and continue to Caxata. About 2 km/ 1¼ mi after Caxata the road forks. The Quime road continues to the right, and the Viloco road drops to the left. Access to all the mountains described below is from the Viloco road. Take a bus or jeep as far as you need to, and get off.

Viloco, the biggest settlement in the area, is a depressing mining village of which Roger Whewell wrote, "the place looked like something from a World War I picture." Viloco's heyday was in the 1920s when it was a prosperous community with its own telephone system and cinema. The Catholic *parroquia* (parish office) offers beds for the night and meals. There are a number of small shops for packaged and fresh food. Gasoline is often available—if not, go to Tienda Pata, a small village 2 km/ 1.25 mi before Viloco.

A jeep from La Paz to Viloco takes 6 to 7 hours and costs US$350. Buses from La Paz to Viloco leave Monday, Wednesday, Thursday, and Saturday at 7:00 A.M., from Calle Jorge Carrasco between Calle 4 and Calle 5, in the El Alto area near La Paz, parallel to the Oruro road. The journey takes 12 hours and costs US$3.30. The return bus from Viloco to La Paz leaves Tuesday, Thursday, Saturday, and Monday at 9:00 A.M.

MAP

IGM Mina Caracoles 6143 III

The mountains of the Quimsa Cruz are listed from north to south.

KORICHUMA
(IMMACULADO)

5,500 m/18,044 ft

SEPTEMBER 1911, THEODOR HERZOG AND CARL SEELIG (GERMANY) FROM THE NORTHWEST

Korichuma is probably the most challenging peak in the area, involving a height gain of almost 1,000 m/3,300 ft from base camp as well as requiring climbers to work a way through a long icefall. The steep snow wall south of the main peak and numerous other lower peaks in the group, most of which are unclimbed, present many new route possibilities. For some reason now unclear, the Aymara peak name is "Golden Jungle" or "Golden River."

Approach

Follow the main road out of the Atoroma valley and over a 4,820 m/ 15,810 ft pass, and then descend. About 8 km/5 mi after the pass, while going around the second sharp curve after the pass, a side road leaves right just past an aqueduct. Follow this road to base camp at the head of Laguna Choco Khota at 4,400 m/14,400 ft.

SOUTHWEST FACE ROUTE

Grade IV/D+, 80°, 900 m/3,000 ft, 9 hours

MAY 1992, DAKIN COOK (U.S.), MARIO MIRANDA (BOLIVIA), AND STAN SHEPARD (U.S.)

From base camp, follow moraine ridges north to reach the start of the glacier in 3 hours. Work a way through the icefall to the base of the Southwest Face. Climb the 10 m/30 ft ice wall (80°), and then continue up through 60° snow to the summit.

Descent: Same. The moraine seems to take even longer on the way down.

ATOROMA

5,565 m/18,258 ft

AUGUST 7, 1928, PEROWITSCH (BOLIVIA) AND JOSEF PREM (GERMANY)

Perowitsch, a workman at the Atoroma mine, was picked by Prem to be his partner on the first ascent of this mountain. One of the major attractions of this peak is the quiet, undisturbed base-camp meadow. In an area unspoiled by major mining activity, wildlife abounds, with pairs of Andean geese flapping and honking and viscachas bounding in and out of the rocky moraine. Clusters of quartz crystals lie around on the ground below the terminal moraine.

KORICHUMA
FROM THE SOUTH

SOUTHWEST FACE ROUTE

DAKIN COOK

ATOROMA
FROM ATOROMA VALLEY

SOUTHEAST RIDGE ROUTE
& DESCENT

SOUTHWEST FACE ROUTE

DAKIN COOK

Approach

As you enter the first valley north of Mina Malla Chuma on the main road to Viloco, head up an unused road to the right that leads to an abandoned mining camp. Base camp is above the alpine meadow.

SOUTHEAST RIDGE ROUTE

Grade II/AD, 50°, 450 m/1,500 ft, 8 hours

AUGUST 7, 1939, PEROWITSCH (BOLIVIA) AND JOSEF PREM (GERMANY)

Go up the moraine north of base camp to the end of the glacier. Head up 40° snow toward a small pyramid-shaped peak between Atoroma and Yaypuri, arriving at a flat part below the unnamed peak. Traverse over to the Southeast Ridge of Atoroma, and follow it to the summit.

Descent: Same

SOUTHWEST FACE ROUTE

Grade II+/AD, 60°, 450 m/1,500 ft, 7 hours

Go up the moraine north of base camp to the end of the glacier. Follow the Southeast Ridge Route to the flat part below the unnamed peak. Cross to the right to the middle of the Southwest Face, and climb the face direct, topping out anywhere along the summit ridge.

Descent: Wander down the northwest ridge toward the small pyramid-shaped peak, then join the ascent route.

GIGANTE GRANDE

5,748 m/18,858 ft

MARCH 6, 1946, FRIEDRICH AHLFELD, GUSTAVO MOELLER, LUCIO MONROY,

DOUGLAS MOORE, EDUARDO SARMIENTO, ERICH SIMON, AND RENÉ ZALLES (BOLIVIA)

This is definitely the most impressive and beautiful massif in the range, and it is almost a roadside mountain. You can easily see it from the road, but it still takes 2 to 3 hours to get in. The West Face requires a wall bivouac for all but the fastest climbers, as well as mixed route ability and equipment. The first and second ascents of the West Face were done within one month in 1993 but, at the time of this writing, the route has not been repeated.

GIGANTE GRANDE
FROM LAGUNA LARAM KHOTA

NORTHWEST RIDGE
ROUTE & DESCENT

WEST FACE ROUTE

DAKIN COOK

Approach

Laguna Laram Khota (literally, "Blue Lake") laps against the side of the main road to Viloco at the small, mostly abandoned settlement of Mina Laram Khota. From the road, follow the path on the southeast side of the lake to the base of Gigante Grande, and camp alongside the San Pedro glacier.

WEST FACE ROUTE

Grade IV (5.6)/D+ (V), 80°, 650 m/2,100 ft, 16 hours

JULY 1993, TEO PLAZA (ARGENTINA) AND IÑAQUI SAN VICENTE (SPAIN)

A small snow cone leads up to a thin ice line that goes through the middle of the face. The ice line is more often formed early in the season rather than later. Above the ice line, a mixed series of pitches at 75° to 80° leads to the upper snowfields (75°). Carry on up the West Face to join the summit ridge to the southeast of the summit. Turn left, and continue to the top.

Descent: Follow the Northwest Ridge down to the San Pedro glacier, and cut back across the bottom of the West Face to base camp.

NORTHWEST RIDGE ROUTE

MARCH 6, 1946, FRIEDRICH AHLFELD, GUSTAVO MOELLER, LUCIO MONROY, DOUGLAS MOORE, EDUARDO SARMIENTO, ERICH SIMON, AND RENÉ ZALLES (BOLIVIA)

From base camp, cross below the West Face to reach the Northwest Ridge, and follow it to the summit.

Descent: Same

JACHA CUNO COLLO
(JACHAKUNUKOLLO, JACHA COLLO, CERRO DON LUIS)

5,800 m/19,029 ft

SEPTEMBER 18, 1939, WILFRID KÜHM AND JOSEF PREM (GERMANY)

OVER THE SOUTHWEST RIDGE

In Aymara, Jacha Cuno Collo is known as "the Big Mountain of Ice," and it is the highest peak in the range. Although Wilfrid Kühm and Josef Prem were the first to reach the top, Theodor Herzog and Carl Seelig got to within 20 m/65 ft of the summit 28 years earlier in 1911. The

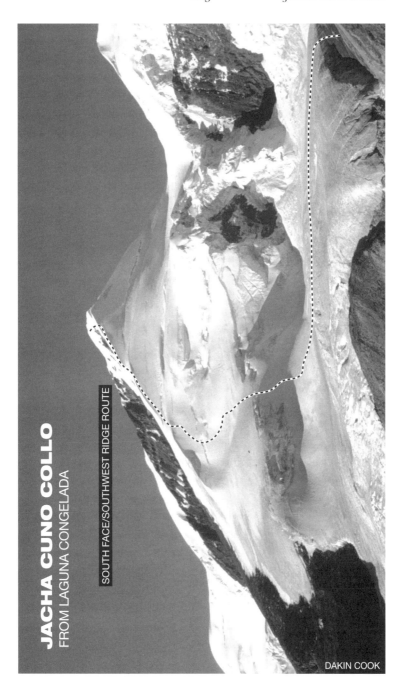

JACHA CUNO COLLO
FROM LAGUNA CONGELADA

SOUTH FACE/SOUTHWEST RIDGE ROUTE

DAKIN COOK

climb is fairly easy, and the best part is the last pitch to the summit. From the southern side, the mountain has a perfect three-part pyramid shape and offers a superb direct variation.

Approach

About 3 km/1¾ miles north of Rodeo, the road forks. Take the lower right-hand fork for about 1½ km/1 mi where a side road crosses a small bridge to the right and enters a valley to the north. Follow this side road, and go up past the Campamento Minero Chojña Khota (literally, "the Green Lake Mining Camp") to reach Laguna Congelada ("Frozen Lake"—it isn't any more) below the glaciers. Camp next to the lake or next to the river below the lake.

SOUTH FACE/SOUTHWEST RIDGE ROUTE

Grade III/AD+, 60°, 650 m/2,100 ft, 7 hours

From Laguna Congelada, go east and up a narrow moraine to the right of the Don Luis, or Chojña Khota, glacier to reach the lower, flat part of the glacier in 1 hour. Traverse due north to reach the 100 m/330 ft south wall (50°). At the top of the wall, go left to the Southwest Ridge (45°) and follow it to a bergschrund 10 m/30 ft below the summit ridge. To avoid the bergschrund, traverse the east face (60°) and move up to the summit ridge.

Descent: Same

HUAYNA CUNO COLLO

5,640 m/18,504 ft

SEPTEMBER 1939, WILFRID KÜHM AND JOSEF PREM (GERMANY)

The Aymara name for this mountain, literally "Little Ice Peak," is in comparison to the higher Jacha Cuno Collo, although the first ascencionists named it Pico Grillo after a mining industrialist who gave them hospitality. The long ridge is a joy to traverse, with occasional arched ice bridges to cross to reach the summit. Photos from the 1920s show the glacier below the peak running into Laguna Huayatani, which is now some distance away from the glacier, showing the extent of glacial retreat in the area.

Approach

From Rodeo on the main road to Viloco, go northeast into the valley of the Monte Blanco mine. Pass the mining camp, and follow the

HUAYNA CUNO COLLO

FROM THE PASS BETWEEN
BASE CAMP AND
THE HUAYATANI BASIN

SOUTH & EAST RIDGE TRAVERSE

DESCENT

DAKIN COOK

valley to the end of the mining road. Base camp is at 4,800 m/15,750 ft, east of the pass which crosses the southwest ridge of San Luis.

SOUTH AND EAST RIDGE TRAVERSE

Grade II/AD, 50°, 550 m/1,800 ft, 6 hours

From base camp, cross west over the pass between Monte Blanco and San Luis to the Huayatani basin and drop down to the Huayatani glacier in 2 hours. Traverse northwest to the 45° ramp that goes up the south face of the ridge. Climb the ramp to the ridge, and then follow the ridge northeast. Traverse over Point 5620 (on the IGM map), and then continue north to reach the summit.

Descent: Go back down until you are above the ramp on the south face of the ridge, and then continue east along the ridge to the top of the Huayatani glacier. Descend south and then back over the pass to base camp.

SAN LUIS

5,620 m/18,438 ft

1982

San Luis together with Jacha and Huayna Cuno Collo are called "Las Tres Marias" by local miners. The combination of a challenging steep lower face leading to a sharp upper ridge, followed by a quick and easy descent, makes San Luis one of the most enjoyable peaks in the area. First reached by the northwest ridge in 1982, the summit can be integrated via this ridge into a grand traverse all the way to Jacha Cuno Collo.

Approach

The approach to and base camp for San Luis are the same as that for Huayna Cuno Collo (see above).

SOUTH FACE ROUTE

Grade III+/D, 70°, 400 m/1,300 ft, 6 hours

JUNE 13, 1993, RANDALL BARNES, DAKIN COOK (U.S.), AND THOMAS MIYAGAWA (BOLIVIA)

From the glacier ½ hour northeast of base camp, climb straight up the south wall on 50° to 70° snow to reach a short mixed section that

SAN LUIS LOWER WALL
FROM THE SOUTH

SOUTH RIDGE DESCENT

SOUTH FACE ROUTE

DAKIN COOK

SAN LUIS RIDGE

SOUTH RIDGE ROUTE
ABOVE SOUTH FACE

FROM THE JUNCTION OF THE LOWER WALL ROUTE
WITH THE SOUTH RIDGE ROUTE

DAKIN COOK

takes you to a ridge at the top of the lower face. From here, follow the sharp 45° south ridge to the summit.

Descent: Go back down the south ridge, follow it west to the pass between San Luis and Monte Blanco, and descend moraine back to base camp.

cordillera occidental

The frost at night split the rocks in the mountainsides into shale,

and it was quite possible, especially in wet conditions, to find

yourself sliding backwards and downwards rapidly, at the same time

as trying to climb forwards and upwards.

Louis de Bernières
The War of Don Emmanuel's Nether Parts, 1990

The Cordillera Occidental is very different from the rest of Bolivia: extinct snowcapped volcanoes rise steeply out of the flat and barren Altiplano. (The smoking volcano to the south is Guallatiri in Chile.) Nights are very cold, habitation is sparse, and life is apparently even harder than in the rest of the country. The harsh landscape is, however, beautiful. Old adobe-brick churches dominate the small villages, and there are *chulpas,* square, adobe-brick, pre-Inca burial chambers. Llamas and vicuñas graze on the plains among *keñua* trees, which are stubby, bushlike, and red barked—the highest trees in the world.

The major problem in the Cordillera Occidental is lack of water. All trips must be planned around the availability of water or proximity to the snow line.

Nieve penitentes *on Sajama, Cordillera Occidental*

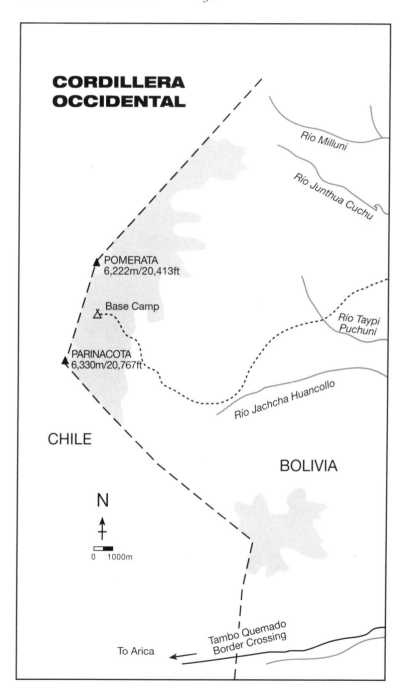

CORDILLERA
OCCIDENTAL

Río Milluni

Río Junthua Cuchu

▲ POMERATA
6,222m/20,413ft

△ Base Camp

Río Taypi
Puchuni

▲ PARINACOTA
6,330m/20,767ft

Río Jachcha Huancollo

CHILE

BOLIVIA

N

0   1000m

To Arica

Tambo Quemado
Border Crossing

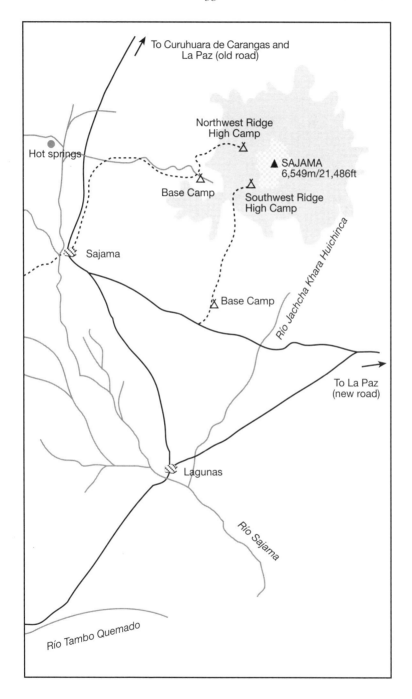

To Curuhuara de Carangas and
La Paz (old road)

Northwest Ridge
High Camp

Hot springs

▲ SAJAMA
6,549m/21,486ft

Base Camp

Southwest Ridge
High Camp

Sajama

Río Jachcha Khara Huichinca

Base Camp

To La Paz
(new road)

Lagunas

Río Sajama

Río Tambo Quemado

Sajama, Bolivia's highest peak, from the Nido de Condores high camp on Illimani in the Cordillera Real

In climbing terms, the greatest hazard is high wind and the greatest inconvenience is the *nieve penitentes* that develop through the season. These vertical pieces of ice can be more than 1 m/3 ft high and make climbing an otherwise easy slope a time-consuming exercise. It is necessary to step around each individual piece of ice because they are too tall to ignore and too strong to crush underfoot. The Bolivian-based German Hans Ertl, who climbed Sajama in July 1951, described the *nieve penitentes* in *Mountain World* (1953) as "knife-sharp ice-stalactites, some over a yard high, which are distributed in close array up to the summit like armoured protection of a modern fortification."

The starting point for the climbs described here is Sajama village, which has no official hotels or restaurants. You must ask around to find somewhere to stay and eat. Start with the office of the Parque Nacional Sajama, where you must register and pay a US$2 park entrance charge. The office can also organize mules and porters. You normally have to arrange the mules the previous day to leave the next morning. A bed for the night costs US$1 and a set dinner *(cena)* costs US$1.20. Very little can be bought in the village beyond dry biscuits, a few canned goods, soft drinks, and beer. Bread is rarely available. Bring all your supplies from La Paz.

Do not miss the hot springs, a 1-hour walk from Sajama village. Soaking in the warm water is a great way to relax after climbing the surrounding volcanoes.

ACCESS

A jeep to the village of Sajama costs US$250 and takes 5 hours via the La Paz–Oruro road as far as Patacamaya, and then on the new asphalt road that goes all the way to Arica in Chile to the east of the volcano Sajama. All international buses to Chile now use this route, so if you take the daily Arica bus that leaves from the main bus terminal in La Paz, you will need to get off at the village of Lagunas and arrange transportation for the 15 km/9 mi to Sajama village. You normally have to pay the full bus fare of US$25, even though you disembark earlier. One bus a week is available from La Paz direct to the village of Sajama; it leaves from Calle Jorge Carrasco, parallel to the Oruro road, in El Alto above La Paz. The bus goes to Lagunas via Curuhuara de Carangas and Sajama village using the old road, on Wednesday at 6:00 A.M. The journey costs US$5 and takes 12 hours or more. The return bus passes through Sajama village on Friday at 2:00 P.M., but the driver stops to sleep in Curuhuara de Carangas, so the return takes 18 hours.

MAPS

Walter Guzmán Córdova Nevado Sajama (this does not include the Payachatas)

IGM Nevado Sajama 5839 IV, Nevados Payachata 5739 II, and Cerro Quisi Quisini 5739 I

SAJAMA

6,549 m/21,486 ft

OCTOBER 4, 1939, WILFRID KÜHM (AUSTRIA) AND JOSEF PREM (AUSTRIA)

(Prem and Piero Ghiglione [Italy] got to within 100–150 m/300–500 ft

of the summit on August 26, 1939.)

Bolivia's highest mountain is 25 km/16 miles from the border with Chile. The normal routes are long and easy, but there are plenty of opportunities for new hard routes, especially early in the season, following ice lines on the rocky west face. It is essential to be acclimatized before attempting Sajama.

Thanks to the new road, Sajama can now be climbed in a long weekend from La Paz—a very different situation from the first attempt in

*Mules ready to go to Camp I on the northwest ridge of Sajama, Cordillera
Occidental*

1927 when it took Josef Prem, an Austrian engineer living in Bolivia, 6
days to reach the mountain from Oruro, 5 of the days riding a mule
"over the dreary, dead Altiplano, under a cold sun and swept by an icy
gale," as he wrote in the *American Alpine Journal* (1943–45).

High winds are a common problem on Sajama, and all high camps
are exposed. During the second (undisputed) successful ascent of
Sajama in 1946, Thomas Polhemus (U.S.) got separated from his com-
panions on the summit plateau in the high winds that whipped up fresh
snow and reduced visibility to 45 m/150 ft. He was never seen again, and
aerial and land searches failed to find any trace of him.

Approach from the West

Day 1: Head north out of Sajama village along the old road to
Curuhuara de Carangas. After 30 minutes, branch off to the right and
gently up. Cross a dry stream, and when you can see the mountain, head
toward it. Cross a wet stream, and then follow it to the right and up to a
broad valley where base camp is located. (Base camp is closer to 4,600 m/
15,100 ft than the 4,700 m/15,400 ft painted on a rock.) A small, clear

bubbling spring provides clean water. Mules to base camp cost US$8, and the trip takes 3 hours from the village.

Day 2: From camp, head across the valley and then follow the path up the slope above. The clear path goes around the hillside to the right and then contours across the base of the mountain before rising to cross a ridge. After the ridge, it is steeper, and the path zigzags up. Earlier in the season the path goes through a snowfield, but later on this is a scree slope. Continue up to high camp at 5,450 m/17,900 ft on the narrow flat spot behind the obvious rock tower to arrive in less than 4 hours from base camp. Porters from base camp to high camp cost US$10 each.

NORTHWEST RIDGE ROUTE

Grade II/AD, 50°, 1,000 m/3300 ft , 6 hours

AUGUST 26, 1939, PIERO GHIGLIONE (ITALY) AND JOSEF PREM (AUSTRIA)

Head up, sticking more or less to the ridge line and avoiding the obvious difficulties. After an hour, do not go up the first snow gullies (unless you enjoy mixed climbing on bad rock) but rather continue across until you reach the bottom of a broad snow gully that leads straight up to a ridge, avoiding all difficulties. The ridge leads to the broad base of the snow dome, although later in the season you must go through a *nieve penitentes* field—the spikes can be 1 m/3 ft high or more. The long, easy angled and seemingly safe snow slopes contain crevasses—some of them quite big. Continue plodding until you reach the highest point on the broad summit plateau.

Descent: Same

■ ■ ■

Approach from the South

Day 1: From Sajama village, follow the road back toward Lagunas, take the left fork, turn left at a small group of houses, and follow the straight track until you arrive at a waterless flat area among *keñua* trees.

Day 2: From the camp, follow paths north up valley toward Sajama's Southwest Ridge. Scree slopes rise to the right toward some red rocks below the glacier. Follow the path up the scree to reach the bottom of a 250 m/800 ft snow slope. Climb the slope to gain a spectacular and airy rock ridge at 5,500 m/18,000 ft. There is space for about six tents at this high camp, which is 6 hours from base camp.

Descending the northwest ridge on Sajama, Cordillera Occidental

SOUTHWEST RIDGE ROUTE

Grade AD/III, 55°, 1,100 m/3,600 ft, 7 hours

From high camp, head up the ice wall. This climb can involve steep ice (60°), but it is normally possible to find a relatively easy way through to reach the snow slopes above. Follow the slopes at a steady 40° to reach the summit plateau. Watch out for crevasses in the seemingly safe snow slopes.

Descent: Same

■ ■ ■

PAYACHATAS
(LOS GEMELOS, "THE TWINS")

These two volcanoes sit to the west of Sajama and mark the border between Bolivia and Chile. If Sajama is Bolivia's Chimborazo, then the perfect cone of Parinacota is Bolivia's Cotopaxi, which has a bigger—although inactive—crater.

The base camp is dry, as are all camps on the Bolivian side of the border. It is necessary to camp as close to the snow line as possible, remembering that this line rises during the season. Take along extra fuel for melting snow. If you make the effort to climb one of the Payachatas, it is worth climbing the other for fantastic views of its nonidentical twin. Chileans climb the Payachatas from Laguna Chungara to the west.

Approach

Head out of Sajama village using the bridge to cross the Río Sajama. The path appears to go way too far to the south, but follow it for the easiest route to base camp. After crossing the Altiplano, the path goes around a series of ridge ends before it heads up to the right into a black sand valley and then stays to the right-hand side of an old lava flow. Stay to the left side of the valley, and head toward the saddle between the two Payachatas until the flat valley floor becomes so narrow that it is only a couple of tents wide. Prem described this area as "extremely desolate and grassless—no bush, no tree. It is filled with volcanic ash and sand, into which one sinks to the ankles." Later in the season, when the snow has been burned off by the sun, it is necessary to go higher up the valley, almost to the saddle, in order to be in reach of snow. Mules to base camp cost US$12 and the trip takes 7½ hours.

The walk out to Sajama village takes 4 hours. The closest running water is 2 hours from camp.

POMERATA
(POMERAPE, POMERATU, PAYACHATA NORTE,
AND HUARMI PAYACHATA)

6,222 m/20,413 ft

MAY 1946, EDMUNDO GARCÍA AND RENÉ ZALLES (BOLIVIA)

Pomerata does not have such a classic shape as its neighbor, but it offers more challenging climbing. The routes are long, and if you are

POMERATA
FROM PARINACOTA

SOUTH RIDGE ROUTE

SOUTHWEST RIDGE ROUTE

attempting some of the more technical lines, an early start is advisable. A compass is necessary to sort out your bearings for the descent.

SOUTHWEST RIDGE ROUTE
Grade II/PD, 45°, 1,000 m/3,300 ft, 7 hours

From base camp, head up to reach the saddle in between Pomerata and Parinacota. Turn right, and move up to join the ridge. Follow the ridge to the summit plateau. Cross the plateau to reach the highest point, which is to the north.

Descent: Same

SOUTH RIDGE ROUTE
Grade III (5.4)/AD+ (III), 50°, 1,000 m/3,300 ft, 8 hours

APRIL 18, 1996, DAVID BANDROWSKI, FELICIA ENNIS, MICHAEL PENNINGS (U.S.)
AND YOSSI BRAIN (U.K.)

This beautiful route offers fantastic views of Parinacota and Guallatiri, the active volcano just over the border in Chile. From base camp facing the saddle between the Payachatas, head up to the right to reach the ridge line in 1½ hours. Follow the ridge line to the end. A rock-scrambling section (5.3/II) and then mixed climbing bring you to the south summit in 6 hours. To reach the true summit takes another 30 minutes. Drop down into a shallow basin, and then head up on the other side.

Descent: Southwest Ridge or, alternatively, from the true summit facing north, go right and down into the valley and up onto the next ridge. Turn right, and continue down.

PARINACOTA
(PAYACHATA, PAYACHATA SUR, MURU PAYACHATA, AND PAYACHATA GRANDE)
6,330 m/20,767 ft

DECEMBER 12, 1928, JOSEF PREM (AUSTRIA) AND TERÁN (BOLIVIA)

Terán was the son of Prem's muleteer, who he picked up on the way to climb Parinacota, the leftmost, cone-shaped, higher of The Twins. The slog up to the snow line is hard effort. Describing the first ascent in the *American Alpine Journal* (1940–42), Prem wrote: "Up we struggled

PARINACOTA
FROM POMERATA

EAST FLANK ROUTE

EAST RIB ROUTE

The long plod up Parinacota, Cordillera Occidental

on the ash cone, inclined at 33 degrees, infinitely painful and causing us to stop for breath after every two or three steps." This scenario has not changed. Because the mountain is classically cone-shaped, all routes are pretty much the same on Parinacota—plod up until you reach the crater rim and find yourself standing on the edge of a 100 m/ 330 ft+ drop.

EAST FLANK ROUTE

Grade I/F, 40°, 800 m/2,600 ft, 6–8 hours

DECEMBER 12, 1928, JOSEF PREM (AUSTRIA) AND TERÁN (BOLIVIA)

Head up to the saddle between the two Payachatas, and turn left. Follow the broad flank straight up until you can distinguish the summit, which is to the north of the crater, and climb it.

Descent: Same

EAST RIB ROUTE

Grade I/F, 40°, 800 m/2,600 ft, 6–8 hours

From base camp, head across sand for 30 minutes to join the rib and scramble up through the friable rock for about 3 hours to reach a flattening where you can rope up and put on crampons. Head straight up, or zigzag depending on your style, for up to 4 hours (depending on the depth of snow) to reach the crater rim. Turn right, and follow the crater rim to the highest point in another 30 minutes.

Descent: Same. Early in the season it is possible to bum-slide from the crater rim and then scree run down the side of the rock rib and be back in camp in under 1½ hours from the summit.

Appendix A

MEDICAL KIT

Many, but not all, of the following drugs can be bought over the counter at pharmacies in Bolivia.

Altitude drugs

Acetazolamide—sustainable release tablets (to be taken prophylactically to help acclimatization; for improved sleep at altitude)

Nefedipine (for High Altitude Pulmonary Edema)

Dexamethasone—pills and injectable plus syringe (for High Altitude Cerebral Edema)

Painkillers

Acetaminofen (Paracetamol)/Aspirin (for headaches)

Ibuprofen (for sprains and muscle aches; not to be used at the same time as ciprofloxacin)

Codeine phosphate (for more serious pain)

Demarol/Temgesic (for broken bones)

Note: Neither codeine phosphate nor Demarol/Temgesic should be used for patients with head injuries as these drugs depress the respiratory system.

Antibiotics

Ciprofloxacin (general and for persistent diarrhea)

Tinidazole (for giardia)

Doxycycline (general)

Co-fluampicil (for broken bones that break through the skin. *Note:* penicillin-based)

Relaxing in the thermal baths after climbing Sajama, Cordillera Occidental

Amoxicillin (for throat, chest, and urinary tract infections. *Note:* penicillin-based)

Erythromycin (broad spectrum nonpenicillin antibiotic)

Other medications

Loperamide (to stop diarrhea when you must travel)

Amethocaine eye drops (for relief of pain, including snow blindness)

clove oil (for relief of tooth pain)

Bonjela (for relief of gum pain)

oral rehydration salts—available at pharmacies, ask for *sales de rehidratación oral* (for diarrhea)

First-aid supplies

space blanket

bandages and elastic bandages

suture strips

adhesive bandages

nonadherent absorbent dressing pads

antiseptic cream

breathable adhesive tape and zinc oxide tape

safety pins

Appendix B

SAMPLE SEVEN-DAY MENU
Based on food available in La Paz (with Bolivian Spanish translation). Portion sizes listed on all packaged foods—especially pasta meals—may not be appropriate (too small).

Breakfast *(Desayuno)*
instant oats *(avena intantanea)*
sugar *(azucar)*
cereal *(cereal)*
powdered milk *(leche en polvo)*
tea/coffee/chocolate *(te/café/chocolate)*

Lunch *(Almuerzo)*
bread *(pan)* for first 4 days
dry biscuits *(galletas de agua)*
tomatoes *(tomates)* for first 2 days
avocados *(paltas)* for first 2 days
mayonnaise *(mayonesa)*
cheese *(queso)*
peanut butter *(mantequilla de mani)* in plastic jars
jam *(mermelada)* in packets
condensed milk with sugar *(dulce de leche)*—this can be spread on bread, added to porridge, or eaten neat
chocolate *(tableta de chocolate)*
peanut and chocolate bars *(Sublime)*
crushed peanut bar *(tableta de mani)*
powdered drink *(refresco en polvo)*—preferably with added vitamin C
dried fruit and nuts *(fruta seca y nueces)*
boiled sweets *(caramelos)*

Dinner *(Cena)*

soup packets *(sopa de sobre)*

dried cheese-filled tortellini *(tortellini relleno con queso)*

Chinese noodles *(fideos chinos)*—2 packets per person per meal

ready-to-eat pasta meals *(comida lista de fideo)*

ready-to-eat rice meals *(comida lista de arroz)*

mashed potato mix *(pure de papa)*

canned cream *(crema en lata)*

canned tomato extract/sauce *(salsa/extrato de tomate en lata)*

garlic salt *(sal de ajo)*

Appendix C

EQUIPMENT LIST
(with Bolivian Spanish translation)

Clothing
balaclava *(pasamontaña)*
thermal top and bottom *(ropa interior termica)*
fleece jacket *(chaqueta de frisa)*
fleece trousers *(pantalones de frisa)*
thin gloves *(guantes delgados)*
inner gloves *(guantes interiores)*
synthetic trousers *(pantalones sintéticos)*
thin synthetic socks *(calcetines sintéticos delgados)*
thick wool socks *(calcetines gruesos de lana)*
shell jacket with integral hood *(chaqueta con capucha)*
mitts *(sobreguantes)*
windproof/waterproof/breathable salopettes/bibs *(overol impermeable)*
gaiters *(polainas)*
plastic boots *(botas plasticas)*
walking boots and socks *(botines y calcetines de caminar)*
sun hat *(sombrero)*

Sun protection
sunscreen *(crema contra el sol)*
100 percent-UV-proof glacier glasses *(gafas con protección UV)*
100 percent-UV-proof ski goggles *(antiparras)*
lip salve *(crema para los labios)*

Climbing supplies
80 liter+ rucksack *(mochila)*
helmet *(casco)*

headlamp with 4.5 volt battery and spare *(linterna frontal y pila de repuesto)*
harness *(arnés)*
12-point crampons *(crampones de 12 puntas)*
ice ax and hammer *(piolet y martillo)*
screwgate and normal karabiners *(mosquetones de seguridad y normales)*
slings *(cintas)*
ice screws *(tornillos de hielo)*
pickets/snow stakes *(estacas de nieve)*
pitons *(pitones)*
50 m x 9 mm rope *(cuerda)*
cord/tape for rappeling *(cordino/cinta para rapel)*
Prussik loops *(nudos Prussik)*
pulley *(polea)*

Camping supplies
down sleeping bag *(saco de dormir de pluma)*
sleeping bag liner *(saco de dormir interno)*
sleeping mat *(aislante)*
tent *(carpa)*
snow pegs *(clavos para nieve)*
bivouac bag *(funda de vivas)*
stove and fuel *(cocinilla y combustible)*
lighters *(encendedores)*
pans, mug, spoon *(ollas, taza, cuchara)*
food *(comida)*
iodine tincture *(iodo)*
1 liter/quart water bottle *(cantimplora)*
4 liter/quart water bag *(bolsa de agua de 4 litros)*

Miscellaneous
medical kit *(botiquín de primeros auxilios)*
penknife *(cortapluma)*
duct tape *(cinta de embalaje)*—not available in Bolivia
map *(mapa)*
compass *(brujula)*
whistle *(silbato/pito)*
money *(dinero)*—in B5 and B10 denomination notes
passport *(pasaporte)*

camera, spare batteries, and spare film *(máquina fotográfica, pilas de repuesto, película)*
notebook, ballpoint pen, and pencil *(libreta, bolígrafo, lapiz)*

Optional:
neoprene face mask *(máscara de Neopreno)*
down jacket *(chaqueta de pluma)*

For longer trips add the following:
sewing kit *(kit de costura)*
extra fuel bottle *(botella de combustible extra)*
spare pick *(punta de piolet de repuesto)*
second rucksack *(segunda mochila)*
book *(libro)*
vitamin C and iron tablets *(tabletas de vitamina C y hierro)*
waterproof stuff sacks *(bolsas impermeables)*
spare laces, gloves, and mitts *(cordones, guantes y sobreguantes extras)*
toothbrush and toothpaste, soap, comb *(cepillo y pasta de dientes, jabón, peine)*

Appendix D

SAMPLE HIRE CONTRACT

Contrato de trabajo **(see translation below)**

Yo, _____, con C.I. _____ me comprometo a realizar el siguiente servicio para _____como porteador / arriero / cocinero / ayudante / guardacampo / chofer

De_____ a _____ ,

    la fecha _____

De_____ a _____ ,

    la fecha _____

De_____ a _____ ,

    la fecha _____

De_____ a _____ ,

    la fecha _____

    Con _____ porteador(es) @ Bolivianos _____ cada uno

    Con _____ mula(s)/llama(s) @ Bolivianos _____ cada una

    Con _____ cocinero(s) @ Bolivianos_____ cada uno

    Con _____ ayudante(s) @ Bolivianos_____ cada uno

    Con _____ guardacampamento(s) @ Bolivianos_____cada uno

    Con _____ movilidad(es) @ US$/Bolivianos _____ para la ida y US$/Bolivianos_____ para la vuelta

    Firma _____   Firma _____

_____   _____ de _____ de _____

(Place of signing)   (day)   (month)   (year)

WORK CONTRACT

I, _____ , I.D. card number _____ promise to carry out the following service for_____ as porter/ muleteer/cook/helper/camp guard/driver

From (place) _____ to (place) _____ ,

    date _____

From _____ to _____ ,

    date _____

From _____ to _____ ,

    date _____

From _____ to _____ ,

    date _____

    With _____ porter(s) @ Bolivianos _____ each

    With _____ mule(s)/llama(s) @ Bolivianos _____ each

    With _____ cook(s) @ Bolivianos _____ each

    With _____ helper(s) @ Bolivianos _____ each

    With _____ camp guard(s) @ Bolivianos _____ each

    With _____ jeep(s) @ US$/Bolivianos _____ for the outward journey and US$/Bolivianos _____ for the return

    Signed _____ Signed _____

_____ _____ of _____ of _____

(Place of signing, e.g., La Paz)   (day)   (month)   (year)

Appendix E

FURTHER READING

Climbing
The main sources of information on which routes have been climbed are the *American Alpine Journal, Alpine Journal,* and the following mountaineering libraries, which are open to the public by appointment only:

Alpine Club Library, 55 Charlotte Road, London EC2A 3QT, U.K.; telephone 0171 613-0755

American Alpine Club Library, 710 10th Street, Suite 15, Golden, CO, U.S.A. 80401; telephone 303-384-0112

Ecole Nationale de Ski et d'Alpinisme, 35 route du Bouchet, B.P.24, 74401 Chamonix, France; telephone 450 55 30 30

Servei General d'Informació de Muntanya, Apartat de Correus 300, E-08200, Sabadell, Spain; telephone 93 723 8413

Hendel, Fred. *Mountains in Bolivia*. Ypsilanti, Mich.: Aventura Press, 1992. A very personal and readable account of climbing in Bolivia in the 1940s and 1950s, with comments on Hans Ertl and other contemporaries climbing in the country.

Mesili, Alain. *La Cordillera Real de los Andes—Bolivia*. La Paz: Los Amigos del Libro, 1984, reprint 1996. A dated but interesting guidebook in Spanish, covering many hard routes done by the French-born author in the 1970s. It is sobering to look at the Mesili topo photographs and compare the level of glaciation he enjoyed with what is left today.

Neate, Jill. *Mountaineering in the Andes: A Sourcebook for Climbers*. 2nd ed. London: Royal Geographic Society, 1994. A reference book listing information on recorded first ascents and new routes. An essential starting point for further research on climbing in Bolivia and the rest of the Andes. *Note:* The first edition has better references.

Pecher, Robert, and Walter Schmiemann. *Die Königskordillere: berg- und skiwandern in Bolivien*. Munich: Christoph and Michael Hofbauer, 1983. The German edition is better than the English edition, which was published in 1977 as *The Southern Cordillera Real*. The stick diagrams used to portray access were difficult to interpret. The guide covers many short, weekend excursions from La Paz.

Medical

Pollard, Andrew, and David Murdoch. *The High Altitude Medicine Handbook*. Oxford and New York: Radcliffe Medical Press, 1997. Clear, detailed, readable, and with some really nasty pictures of frostbite. Everything the high-altitude climber needs to know about medicine. (Also available in Micro Edition weighing 60g/2 oz.)

Wilderness Medical Society. *Practice Guidelines for Wilderness Emergency Care*. William Forgey, M.D., ed. Indiana: I.C.S. Books Inc., 1995. This most readable wilderness medical guide includes specific chapters on high-altitude illness, hypothermia, and frostbite as well as other sorts of illnesses and injuries possible in the outdoors.

Wilkerson, James, M.D., ed. *Medicine for Mountaineering*. 4th ed. Seattle: The Mountaineers, 1992. Without doubt, the most comprehensive book on mountain medicine—it's over 400 pages long, but worth reading before you go on a trip.

General

Box, Ben, ed. *South American Handbook*. Bath: Footprint Handbooks, annual. The most up-to-date general guidebook—updated every year—covering the whole of the continent.

Cramer, Mark. *Culture Shock! Bolivia*. Portland, Ore.: Graphic Arts Center, 1996. A personal account of customs and etiquette, history and politics, economics and culture, written by a U.S. journalist living in Bolivia.

Hendel, Fred. *Revolutions in Bolivia*. Ypsilanti, Mich.: Aventura Press, 1992. A personal account of living in Bolivia from 1939 to the 1960s, written by an Austrian emigrant who witnessed and investigated various important and interesting events, including the public lynching of President Villaroel, the Black Friday massacre, and the 1952 national revolution, among others.

Kunstaetter, Robert, and Daisy Kunstaetter, eds. *The Latin American Travel Advisor*. Quito, Ecuador: Latin American Travel Consultants, (rku@ecnet.ec). Travelers' intelligence quarterly newsletter covering public safety, health risks, economics, politics, and travel costs for Bolivia and 16 other Latin American countries.

Murphy, Alan, ed. *Bolivia Handbook*. Bath: Footprint Handbooks, 1998. The most up-to-date general guidebook to the country, updated every two years.

Swaney, Deanna. *Bolivia: A Travel Survival Kit*. 3rd ed. Australia: Lonely Planet, 1996. The most detailed general guidebook to the country.

Van Lindert, Paul, and Otto Verkoren. *Bolivia in Focus*. London: Latin American Bureau, 1994. Short, well-designed, and very readable study of the people, history, politics, economy, and culture of Bolivia.

Index

Page numbers in boldface indicate topos. Page numbers in italics indicate maps.

About the Author

Yossi Brain topping out on the summit of Huayna Potosí, having climbed the 1,000m/3,300 ft west face (Photo by Gerry Arcari)

While recovering in the intensive care unit of a Chamonix hospital following an 800 m/2,600 ft fall in the French Alps, Yossi Brain decided to quit his job as a political reporter for an evening newspaper in Britain and take up climbing full time. He moved to Bolivia where he works as a mountain and trekking guide and runs the Ozono adventure tourism agency in La Paz. Brain is the first (and only) non-Bolivian member of the Bolivian Association of Mountain Guides. A member of the American Alpine Club and the South American Explorers Club, he is former climbing secretary of the Club Andino Boliviano. He spends as much time as possible climbing and also indulges in a bit of freelance journalism. He is resident Bolivia correspondent for the *South American Handbook,* and is also the author of *Trekking in Bolivia: A Traveler's Guide.*

Born in 1967, he has climbed in countries on three continents, and extensively in Ecuador where he goes to avoid the Bolivian wet season.

THE MOUNTAINEERS, founded in 1906, is a nonprofit outdoor activity and conservation club, whose mission is "to explore, study, preserve, and enjoy the natural beauty of the outdoors. . . . " Based in Seattle, Washington, the club is now the third-largest such organization in the United States, with 15,000 members and five branches throughout Washington State.

The Mountaineers sponsors both classes and year-round outdoor activities in the Pacific Northwest, which include hiking, mountain climbing, ski-touring, snowshoeing, bicycling, camping, kayaking and canoeing, nature study, sailing, and adventure travel. The club's conservation division supports environmental causes through educational activities, sponsoring legislation, and presenting informational programs. All club activities are led by skilled, experienced volunteers, who are dedicated to promoting safe and responsible enjoyment and preservation of the outdoors.

If you would like to participate in these organized outdoor activities or the club's programs, consider a membership in The Mountaineers. For information and an application, write or call The Mountaineers, Club Headquarters, 300 Third Avenue West, Seattle, Washington 98119; (206) 284-6310.

The Mountaineers Books, an active, nonprofit publishing program of the club, produces guidebooks, instructional texts, historical works, natural history guides, and works on environmental conservation. All books produced by The Mountaineers are aimed at fulfilling the club's mission.

Send or call for our catalog of more than 300 outdoor titles:

The Mountaineers Books
1001 SW Klickitat Way, Suite 201
Seattle, WA 98134
1-800-553-4453
e-mail: mbooks@mountaineers.org
website: www.mountaineers.org